POSITIVE POWER 2

-DISCOVERING YOUR SPIRIT &
Finding your way back Home

by

RAJ D.RAJPAL

B.Sc.(Hons.), G.C.E.(Cambridge), M.B.A.(Ohio)

PIONEER COMMUNICATION

PIONEER COMMUNICATION

SHOWCASE OF SELF-IMPROVEMENT BOOKS

You have it all now-your Life is truly yours to discover & Enjoy
Quantum Public Speaking
Positive Thinking for Teenagers
Positive Power 1

FORTHCOMING BOOKS

The Power of Attraction
Unconditional Meditation
Unconditional Love

POSITIVE POWER 2

-DISCOVERING YOUR SPIRIT
and finding your way back Home

by

RAJ D.RAJPAL

B.Sc.(Hons.), G.C.E.(Cambridge), M.B.A.(Ohio)

Coach and Public Speaker
Trainer, Bob Proctor Motivation program
Canadian National Quality Award Recipient
Platform Speaker, Yoga and Meditation discourses
Trainer, Bob Proctor Advanced Motivation program

Best selling author:
"Quantum Ethics"
"Positive Power 1"
"Positive Thinking for Teenagers"
"You have it all now, your Life is truly yours to discover and enjoy."

PIONEER COMMUNICATION
www.thepioneercommunication.com

PUBLISHER:

PIONEER COMMUNICATION

Orders for additional books can be placed at:

rajrajpal@yahoo.com

National Library of Canada

Rajpal Raj D., 1951-

Positive Power 2/Raj D. Rajpal

Includes Index

ISBN: 978-1-9990902-0-3

This book is dedicated to all spiritually minded individuals, who strive to find their true Calling and Purpose of Life and are motivated to live a richer, more Positive Life by developing better relationships with others. These blessed individuals will truly find their way back Home--- into a blissful center of Harmony, Love and Happiness.

TABLE OF CONTENTS

PART 1

INTRODUCTION

"If you look for the truth outside yourself,
it gets further and further away,
Today, walking alone
I meet him everywhere I step,
He is the same as me,
yet I am not him.
Only if you understand it in this way,
will you merge with the way things are".

- Tung Shan (807-869)

Life is all about Relationships. We have and maintain relationships with ideas, things, Nature and most importantly, with People who co-exist within our Natural Surroundings. Nothing exists in a vacuum and ideas, feelings and perceptions are all in relationship to something, whether this relationship trigger is caused by an external event or through an internal perception or reaction (to experiences of the past, present or projected future).
This book, entitled, "Positive Power 2", takes off after an earlier best-selling publication, "Positive Power 1"----- it builds on a continuation of the story of Relationships.

Therefore, when we think about Positive Power, derived through our right understanding of relationships, we also need to look at this Power in a new and unique way. Power is derived out of an understanding and optimal management of our relationships; therefore, "Positive Power 2," is written in story book format expounding our various relationships with our thoughts, emotions and other Life interactions. This new publication attempts to explain and elucidate how an individual can gather and accentuate Personal Power by understanding how he relates to his Life through expression of a myriad of Relationships, and his reaction to them, whether positive or negative.

And since Life is nothing but a series of Relationships, some causing happiness and a lot creating pain and isolation, this book reflects on how we are affected by external and internal psychological events. The story book setting then talks about common responses to Life Events and how a good and clear understanding of these Events can assist one live a happier and more complete Life.

"Life events," in the context of this book, are presented as relationships to specific attitudes, actions and behavior as they relate to different circumstances we face in our every day Life. The author takes great care in looking at the effects of some of the substantial Life relationships experienced. Through this connection with Relationships and its after- effects, both sweet and bitter, there is a meaningful discussion on how to uplift yourself and develop Positive meaning and Purpose in one's Life. The net result of this Awareness and Self-Knowledge culminates in the ushering of a wiser and simpler Life, filled with much Happiness and Love. And do Happiness and Love not constitute the most important things we seek as we live in a tumultuous, volatile world?????

It is the author's prayer and steadfast intention, to assist the reader to discover this wellspring of happiness and balance within oneself.

THE STORY OF LIFE

Life is indeed mysterious. We come into this World from an unknown Source of Consciousness. Having no choice in the selection of our parents or natural environment, we are forced into this world and have to adapt to changing circumstances, many of which we are not responsible for. In order to survive, both physically and mentally, we are forced to assimilate and adopt the values of our family and immediate culture and proceed through distinct Life cycles in stages; first, starts the birth and education period, followed by the second period of career building/professional development and simultaneously a third period of marriage, which may involve raising a family and finally the last period of rest and retirement. Through all of these mysterious and unknown stages, we attempt to find meaning and purpose in our Life.

Our Lives are often touched with Grace and love, but at the same time subject to much change and volatility as we strive to impose our views and expectations on others in our quest of fulfilling our Life destiny. Karmic forces pre-determine, in many instances, our exposure to different situations and challenges. However, the control of your Life rests solely in your own hands. Man has the capacity and power to change his Destiny and Future. Very few are successful in this process of utilizing their innate Power to Change. For these blessed individuals, the achievement of Purpose is easy. However, for most of us, Life is a long and challenging trip, which gets very frustrating at times. At many times in our Life, we may lose Hope and Confidence in our ability to change things around us to fulfill our personally crafted Purpose. As our Life cycle changes, we go through adjustment challenges as we strive to create the perfect balance between home and work, between Love and Social Service, between our needs and the expectations of others close and dear to us.

As we move through this incredible Life Adventure, I wonder how many really look at Life events as they effect one from a purely impersonal point of view. Is it possible to view your Life from the outside as a total stranger to your own very personal thoughts, feelings and experiences? Could you imagine living, (even for a few moments) outside your "mental and emotional" bubble, while simultaneously watching your Life grow and develop from without?

For most of us, this is difficult; it seems almost impossible to maintain this detachment, since we are so tied to the results of what we seek and limited by our narrow self-indulgent view of Life. If there was some way of stepping out of our usual Life box of experiences and feelings therefrom, while impersonally surveying our relationships with different ideas, things and people then this might allow us to re-calibrate and re-align our Life so we may fulfill what we believe we need, which would then in turn lead to less stress and more happiness.

Meditation and self-awareness are great ways of finding that impersonal observation of your Life Experience. Happiness is what we seek but unfortunately the way we try to achieve it creates more conflict and pain. So is there a way out of this dilemma? Why do we, as rational humans, self-destruct our peace and happiness?

This book hopes to give you a new unbiased, impersonal view of your Life. A few chapters on Meditation and intensive introspection will assist in poly-angular impersonal attention, which will create a wellspring of Happiness and Peace within. And this will be achieved by understanding and harnessing your Personal Power through understanding of all your Relationships. Can you be impersonal and yet simultaneously live personally with your Life experiences? Although this appears to be paradoxical on the surface----- to me, this is the only true way to get outside yourself and watch your Life in total 360 degree vision.

Life is very short and one has so little time to self-explore. Before one knows one's Precious Life has passed and one is gone from this World. With all the responsibilities of education, career and the challenge of finding True Love and raising a family with additional financial responsibility for saving enough for retirement, there seems to be so little time to be quiet.

This book attempts to encourage and motivate you to understand Life impersonally. A quiet, detached observation of your Life, assisted with Meditation, Contemplation and Poly-angular attention will open the way to a better Life for You.

MISSION STATEMENT

This book takes on an unusual approach. Instead of propounding the value of Positive Thinking, it goes beyond that concept to a value proposition of Positive Power, derived with the assistance of Positive thinking but on a macrocosmic scale. "Positive Power" is defined as harnessing, growing and maintaining your personal power. The concept of Positive Power combines the strength of Positive Thinking with the spiritual clarity resulting in fulfillment of your self-determined Purpose in Life. Positive thinking by itself cannot solve all of Life's challenges. It may help in the achievement of material goals, which are important for the economic and financial sustenance of Human Life. However, there are other more important callings in Life. And these callings deal with the achievement, maintenance and growth of Love, Happiness and Self-Realization.

As we humans live and strive for excellence, we meet with resistance and much sorrow in our lives, due to an unfulfillment of our desires. Therefore, in order to progress more effectively and efficiently, we need to find a way of integrating Positive Thinking with Positive Power. And this Power can only be discovered and harnessed through intensive internal observation and contemplation, guided by Meditation and 24/7 choice-less awareness of our Life circumstances. Positive Thinking teaches you to never give up, however difficult your Life circumstance may be; Positive Power teaches you to live and face every situation with total understanding and Purpose. Therefore Positive Thinking can make you rich, yet unhappy and unfulfilled---- however Positive Power will transcend this situation and discover your true relationship with things, ideas and People. Happiness and Balance are natural by-products of this new found Positive Power.

So, this book, in story book format, talks about our attitudes, which affect our relationships with Life situations. Some of these attitudes and subsequent relationships deal with how we face aging, anger, anxiety, bitterness, among other situations in Life. The author discusses how most people assess their relationship with these ideas, attitudes and resulting situational experiences. We move on to shed a light on how self-observation, meditation and awareness can create a new Light and understanding in daily Living.

The sole objective of this book remains the enlightenment and true understanding of your purpose in Life and how you may, irrespective of your current situation, stay happy 24/7, while at the same time maintain your dedication and Success to whatever Life pursuit you choose. This book does not have the intention of indoctrinating you in any shape, form or manner or forcing you to adopt consciously or sub-consciously any religious or dogmatic belief. This book's purpose is simple: to assist you in becoming a more balanced, integrated and spiritually aware human being.

It is the author's intention that as more and more humans get enlightened with this new view on Life, that this new Spirit of Understanding and Self-Realization spreads through the World, thereby creating a new World Economic and Spiritual Order. Civilization is at a tilting point and has now reached a stage where we Humans either take on this challenge of co-existing happily or otherwise move, by default, towards the road to violence and ultimate self-destruction.

The author has written this book to spread the word of Peace and Wisdom. Should you want to improve your Life and achieve what you wish, while at the same time maintain your happiness 24/7, then this book could be a valuable tool to accomplishing this noble purpose.

PART 1

THE STORY OF RELATIONSHIPS (A-Z) AS THEY APPLY TO IDEAS, SITUATIONS AND LIFE EVENTS

AGING

The concept of Age varies from culture to culture. In the ancient Hindu civilization, which exists in India for three thousand years, the concept of Age was delineated quite chronologically; the religious texts showed four different Life stages---- the First being birth and education, the second that of Marriage and raising a family, while the Third was career and business development followed by the final stage, which was meant to be dedicated towards simplicity and spiritual fulfillment. As times changed and new pressures were exerted by Civilization and Technology, the understanding, perception and experience of Aging made a dramatic u turn.

In the Western World, Age is initially associated with youth and vitality. As we progress through Life's incredible journey, our attitudes and opinions shift, too. From a purely physical point of view, many Western women, crave for a young and beautiful bodily expression; endless amount of dollars are being spent in grooming her body, adorning it with make-up and fragrances and rich, sensuous clothes. To this Woman, a youthful look appreciably increases her chances of attracting and maintaining attention from the opposite sex. It also helps her maintain the attention of her loved one or spouse.

Is Perception of Age determined solely by an applied standard of external beauty? Does this beautification and greater attention provide a better Peace? And what about Inner Beauty? Dr. Maxwell Maltz, in his classic book, "Psycho-Cybernetics," shares numerous examples of patients who came to have plastic surgery in his clinic. Their purpose was to simply beautify their bodies. Some wanted a more prettier, well shaped nose while others wanted breast augmentation. And, in many instances, their craving for a better physique was tied in to their lack of inner confidence and poor self-esteem.

It is true that physical aging is a natural process, but is it crucial to pay such singular and undivided attention to it as if your very Life depended on it? And what about inner Aging? Has anyone given thought to this? When Life continues over a long period of time, chronologically, are you living every day of your Experience the same way, accompanied with the same habits and mode of action? Such repetition makes the mind dull and accentuates the physical aging process.

So can your relationship with Aging be different? Can you view the physical part of the body, which reduces bodily function with age, as a natural process and focus more attention to your inner aspect, which is the real important relationship? Can you also come in touch with your extreme inner aspect of consciousness? Do you possess a quality or spirit, which never dies? And do you see the difference between this Spirit and your usual Mind with its desires and cravings? Does that Spirit ever age? If your relationship with Aging is consistent with the fear of dying as you physically decay, then you have set up a catastrophic living hell for yourself. If on the other hand, you view Life as a progression of happy and changing Experience, with complete confidence that you can face all challenges positively, then your Relationship with Aging has changed.

You now see yourself as a pulsating Light, a deep and powerful Energy Center, nourished by the Spirit within and strengthened by your Mind and Inner Resolve, moving forward to the Ultimate Bright Light from which we originated and to which we merge on Death. Then Physical Aging has no real meaning. Your Relationship with this concept changes and you become more a Person who lives in simplicity, on a moment-to-moment basis.

So establishing the right relationship with aging and death, becomes most crucial to the discovery of Inner Happiness. Change your Relationship with Aging and you instantly Change your Life. Make your Life more meaningful and bright. Make that precious Gift called Life more of a positive challenge. And move towards the Positive Power. Move in tandem with the Universal Light in every moment of your Existence. You do have a choice: either to stay stuck in repetitive opinions, attitudes and actions or start your journey towards becoming a Positive Agent of Change by incorporating and moving with that Transcendent Light 24/7.

ANGER

Anger is a very strong human emotion. And it can help you harness the Power to do good. However, more likely, we use it to inflict pain on others. So before we can discuss our Relationship with Anger, we must understand how Anger is caused.

The human Mind has, deep within itself, a deep and lingering need for fulfillment. And this fulfillment expresses itself in the form of Desire. Such desire is usually to accomplish a pre-determined and valuable need or to acquire a certain sensation or experience. And when that desire gets stymied or blocked in its fulfillment, a Mental Reaction, sets in. Anger is one form of expression of such unfulfilled desire or need. Anger is then accompanied by violence, whether such violence be expressed psychologically or through physical actions.

So if we understand that we are all prone to be unfulfilled at various stages of our Life, is it fair to be subservient to Anger in our relationships with our loved ones? Before we try to mend our broken or incomplete relationships with loved ones, should we not first try to understand ourselves and what is making us Angry?

The typical relationship with Anger is as follows:

1. I want or need something to feel more fulfilled.

2. I am not able to accomplish this feeling or fulfillment in my relationship with another, whether this other be a person or situation. My wife or girlfriend made me happy for a little while. And now, I am turned off, because she did not do or say something I wanted her to.

3. This non-fulfillment triggers an angry sensation in my Psyche. I may feel a gush of negative energy flow through my System accompanied with an uncontrollable urge to express this negativism in talk or action. My blood pressure may shoot up and I might feel a cold flush or an angry sensation which needs to be vented immediately.

4. I therefore, to throw out physically, this ugly sensation and feeling, say or act in a very negative and crude manner.

5. The effect of this crudity creates a greater negative ripple due to resistance and argument from the other, resulting in a loss of communication or total collapse of a relationship.

Now, the challenge here is, whether it is possible to come face-to-face with this Anger and stop it from creating a destructive relationship. So instead of focussing on who did what wrong, one shifts attention to the Anger itself.

This is initially a very challenging exercise. But as you do this, your Attention and Energy shifts from being negative, emotionally to a neutral emotional point and later, with sufficient practice and self-awareness to a Positive Energy Emotion.

The key here is to be able to understand yourself better and be more aware of your unfulfilled need. Is instantaneous fulfillment of that need, really important enough for you to express your anger and harm a beautiful relationship? If you change your relationship with Anger, by not allowing it to vent itself instantaneously, you now create a Gap or space between yourself and the Anger. By allowing yourself to live and breathe in that Space, however momentarily that might be, you allow a Quiet, Peaceful Power to gather in your System and that Power can and will bring more quietness in your Being and allow you to control your negative expression of Anger. Change your Relationship with Anger and you have taken the first step to changing your Life. Happiness and Understanding will follow and the relationship will be repaired with the other person or situation.

In a relationship with another, your peace of mind and non-reaction (to what the other person says or does), in the presence of a volatile argument or situation, will by itself, tame the other person's negative response. And that will set up the right environment for a discussion of any problem you might have. A fundamental change occurs when you do not take your Anger very seriously, but use it as a tool to garner more Love and Attention. This is the conviction tool discussed next. Love always wins in any relationship and it now becomes a challenge to focus on Love rather than Anger, however much the justification for Anger may be.

The other side of Anger is conviction. Let me explain. You are on a project of self-improvement in your Life and some of the friends in your natural circle do not appreciate your effort or changed attitudes. As it is in dedicated and committed social networks, the individual is dragged down to the lowest common denominator of the entire group. So if you want to stand out and are convinced of your Purpose in Life, you now hold your ground steadfastly. So Anger, which is basically internalized, is used to fortify your defense of your Values. Anger now becomes an ally of inner conviction. The use of Anger is to bolster your Value System.

In this limited application only does Anger have any value. Otherwise, Anger generally results in broken relationships, violence and external and internal discord and therefore the outer manifestations of Anger need to be controlled. Understand yourself, take things easy and accept that there is Anger bubbling, quite spontaneously, at different points of time in your relationship with others. By not allowing it to express itself, you will exhibit behavior exhibited by the top one per cent of the population--- the really true Self Actualizers. Now you are in Presence of Anger, yet free from it. You have sublimated yourself emotionally to use energy positively to fulfill your Life Purpose.

Change that relationship with Anger and this will change the way others look at you as you become a more confident, peaceful and happy person. The focus is now on your relationship with anger and not how or why it is caused, or who is causing it. Change your focus and you will immediately and instantaneously change the way you view yourself. This changed view will garner more positive feelings from everyone around you. Change your relationship with Anger and you have one more step towards changing your Life by becoming a happier, self-actualized person.

ANXIETY

Anxiety is a very common human phenomenon. And for those who cannot deal with it effectively, it can lead to deeper and more intense psychological reactions like neurosis, psychosis, schizophrenia and also at the worst level of violence, in suicidal tendency. Unfortunately, we humans have learned to react very quickly at the first signs of anxiety: instead of trying to understand its origin, we rush to react to it, through symptomatic influences.

The "flight or fight" response so brilliantly expounded by Canadian psychiatrist, Hans Selye, come to mind here. Let me briefly expound. When there is the fear of the unknown, expressed through anxiety, there is an immediate fight or flight response. The human organism either gets ready to confront and fight (against the situation or imaginary projection causing the fear) or it tears out in a hurry to escape from any intended result, whether real or imaginary. But must we not understand the root cause of anxiety rather than yield to the "fight or flight" response?

What causes this anxiety reaction? To fully understand the nature of anxiety, we must delve into the deeper portions of the Mind. The Mind, through Thought mechanism, is the response in real time to memory (facing any given situation). Such situation could be real or imaginary. The Mind, moves through three stages, when confronted with an anxious situation or event: the past, the present and the future. Although we are all exhorted to live in the moment, very few us really achieve this state of consciousness. We are constantly moving through our past expressions, opinions and experiences and projecting the results of our current goals and desires into the future. When we perceive a threat to our way of Life or our established way of doing things or to our deepest and fondest desires, the fear of loss triggers the symptoms which follow the onset of anxiety.

Fear, desire and anxiety are very closely linked and at some point of time in the book, we will contemplate on this important connection. For now, let us try to understand our response to anxiety; triggered by a known or unknown, undesirable external or inner thought impulse, we act to protect ourselves against a real or projected/imagined reality. The moment we experience a loss of a loved one, which is a real and present danger, we go into a shell and feel emotionally distraught and isolated.

This can further lead to negative physical symptoms, like accentuated blood pressure, loss of appetite and even severe cardiac and other bodily reactions. The thread which connects our mind and body is very subtle. The body reacts to the signals sent by the Mind. When the Mind is happy, relaxed and stable, the body embellishes in this beauty of emotional grandeur. On the other hand, when the Mind is disturbed, those psychological vibrations ripple into a negative bodily state, which is a state of dis-ease.

So what is the right relationship between you and Anxiety? Is Anxiety caused by something outside you? Or do you cause it by your approach and reception to change and the unknown? Can you control the symptomatic "fight/flight," response or are you a Pawn in the ever changing game of Life, sometimes happy, sometimes fighting, sometimes worried. Are you willing to accept the ups and down of your psychological moods or do you want to control this? And how do you control this? By fighting, by adopting some religious mantra? Or is there an easier way to live a Life beyond Anxiety and Pain?

First and foremost, you must learn to meditate. And by this, I do not mean the kind of meditation being taught in American mainstream society. Nor should one want to follow the traditional type of meditation of the East. These methods and techniques will, at the most, give you temporary relief but not result in an understanding of the whole dimension of Anxiety. And unless you understand the entire origin and expression of Anxiety, you will not be able to rise beyond its negative psychological and physical manifestations.

If you understand Meditation as a passive, choice-less awareness process and you put in the time and effort to see the Anxiety when it first arises in your thought process, then you have taken the first step to dealing with the negative effects of Anxiety. Quiet, introspective attention of the origin of Anxiety and the acceptance of the "fight/flight autonomous response," will help. By this, I mean, that you do not become part and parcel of the autonomous fight/flight response, but that you merely become aware of the psychological disturbance. You then look at the situation polyangularly and then determine what the best course of action is to rise beyond the Anxiety response. Is the Anxiety caused by a real or imaginary situation? Can you detach yourself, even if momentarily, from the situation to see the situation in a totally unbiased manner? The more space you create between the Anxiety and yourself, the more clearer the picture will become.

And then you adopt a plan of action, which best meets with that external challenge. And that is it. When the anxiety arises after a decision is made, you merely acknowledge its presence but remain detached from the process. The less attention you give to Anxiety, the more in control you are.

Anxiety is a burning issue in this World and its effects are felt worldwide. Men kill each other, while projecting that there is somehow, a loss of one's way of Life due to someone else (a declared enemy) possessing the means to destroy them. In most cases, these opinions and feelings are misjudged. But the violence and hurt caused to others is irreversible.

Love and understanding will solve the relationship with Anxiety. If you learn to forgive more, if you stay calm and accepting of the present moment, which is ever changing, if you meditate more intensely with poly-angular attention, the Anxiety itself metamorphoses into something different--- you now create a Peaceful Zone in your Life, one which is untouched by all the travails and tensions initiated by Anxiety.

BITTERNESS

A bitter heart does no one any good. And the quality of bitterness, accompanied with violence in thoughts, actions and behavior seems to abound everywhere. It feels so easy to be angry and scorn another; it is sometimes comfortable to criticize or look down on the other. It therefore serves as a tool of self-aggrandizement, which strokes the individual Ego. Finding fault with someone else's behavior seems to be a common pastime. We all live in our own "bubble of ideas, pre-conceived judgments and values" and we look at the world through such colored glasses of opinion and experience. It is as if we believe, falsely, that we have a Divine right to judge others--- but do we really have the right to judge, holding our image as the perfect image of Life?

Bitterness also expresses itself through failed or unfulfilled Life Experiences. You have invested your emotions in someone you loved; that person has forsaken you. You feel bitter at the sudden change of affairs. In your mind's eye, you were looking for a more perfect union. You wanted so much to continue enjoying the pleasure and Love of your Partner. But the object of your desire, the apple of your Eye has now chosen to devote herself to some other person. And so, even though your relationship is finished, the bitterness still exists deep down in your Psyche. And you carry this bitterness around. It is a venom, which devours other associations, destroying your chance to find happiness elsewhere.

Or, in another situation, you are passed over for a promotion awarded to another office associate. This was a position you believed you deserved. There is anger and bitterness at the organization, which downgraded your work and this is accompanied by jealousy towards the other associate who has now gone ahead of you. So what is your relationship with failure in any event or situation in Life? Do you view yourself as failing more than winning in Life? Do your failings snowball into a vast mountain of non-success accompanied by depression and negativism? Do you start losing your Self-Confidence? Or can you look at a failing being of a temporary nature and vastly different than permanent failure, understanding that unless you give yourself permission to fail, you will not eventually succeed? And so could you view tiny failings as a stepping stone to long-term success?

Only you determine what you think and feel, although many people close to you might want to dictate what it means to be a Worldly Success. With all the change we go through, and with the constant demands placed by Life, it is so easy to be bitter about things which went wrong. But if you realize that if you continue to carry the seed of bitterness, you will reproduce in the future, situations, which cause the same failing to happen. Not to mention, the immediate and intense negative emotion and harm this bitterness can produce.

The right relationship with bitterness, is to acknowledge, that this exists as a reaction in everyone's Life. And to consciously work to not allow this bitterness to permeate into your present and future. Conscious awareness, positive visualization and a great confidence that you will be able to live a better Life, moment-to-moment will create the right environment for the annihilation of bitterness. The cure for bitterness is the understanding that any single event cannot and will not effect your Happiness and the denial of bitterness on a 24/7 basis is the solution to a Happier and more Meaningful Life.

BONDAGE

Human Bondage possess a great challenge to most Humans. In days gone by, during the settling of the Americas, which started four centuries back, Africans were captured and kidnapped by European merchants and their protagonists and brought on slave ships to the Americas and other British colonies. Being a cheap source of labour, they were paid little or no wages and forced to work in plantations in the Southern US and Bahamas and Cuba for the profit of rich and conniving landowners and farmers. This was an extreme form of physical and mental bondage where generations of Africans were committed to slavery.

As freedom expressed itself in the West and Africans and other foreign nationals were allowed to own land and move around freely while expressing their opinions, the situation got better for millions of immigrants forced into a new land without their permission, knowledge or authorization. As freedom and wealth flourished in the West, a new form of disease crept up: a disease of loneliness and separation. Although the populace was economically rich (compared to other developing country populations) and relatively healthy due to advances in medicine and technology, there seemed to be a lingering feeling of isolation and loneliness. In a book I read recently, the author suggested that "men lived in beautiful and comfortable homes, but were living in prisons of their own choosing." These were not physical prisons, but a self-enclosed and frustrated mental and emotional prison formed by our inability to connect happily with the communities and businesses we interacted with. With social disintegration and divorced families in Western Society, Life suddenly became treacherous and lonely. So we, in the West, created prisons in our Mind---- these were Prisons of our choosing. So physical bondage four centuries back, got supplanted with Mental Bondage today. These Prisons were more subtle: they had to do with how we felt about ourselves and our relationship with the world at large. There was now a new form of Bondage---- a Mental Bondage which created frustration, loneliness and separation. And most unfortunately this was a type of Prison, of which we were not 24/7 aware, and also one where a majority of the affected population did not take preemptive steps (to surpass the bad reactions and results thereof).

So what is Mental Bondage? It is adherence to a way of Life, which is not consistent with one's adjustment to the World at large. You hold a certain set of values and cherish certain desires, which have not been fulfilled or dream of good experiences that once existed but now are gone.

What is one to do here to escape from this frustration and tension? Drink more alcohol? Go on a drug spree? Have incessant fights with our loved ones? Or commit suicidal acts and other acts of violence? All of these are bad options for healthy living.

I guess, the first step, is to seriously devote time and energy to understand, appreciate and accept that Human Bondage is not a must, nor is it essential. Secondly, to understand and implement a system of Life, where you can defeat the Feeling of Bondage itself. If you feel you have no hope of surpassing the ill-effects of bondage, then you never will. And if you believe you can, you will. Another suggestion is not to be too attached to anything, or to any one single outcome, but to Live Life to the fullest, believing you will attract what you deserve, even though this may take time for fruition.

An additional idea is to seriously and sincerely look at your Life, and analyze, and pay attention to the way you treat yourself and others, searching for a better behavior pattern to improve not only your Life but others. Another important concern is the two levels of discernment of Bondage: one, I would like to call Competent Bondage and the other one Incompetent Bondage.

Competency deals with the level of awareness of what is disturbing you at any particular point of time. Competent bondage, refers to your awareness of the fact that you, as a human being, feel that sense of Bondage. You feel stymied in your efforts to get what you want or feel cheated of a good relationship, through no perceived fault of your own. You also feel that in spite of your awareness of this feeling of Bondage, you do not have the Power or Ability to change things around you to get what you believe you deserve.

A more dangerous form of Bondage, is the variety called, "Incompetent Bondage." In this psychological state, you feel constricted but do not really know what is causing the discomfort. You therefore try to vent your frustration through anger, violence and ill-will both to yourself and to others, both near and far from you. This type of Bondage has no immediate cure, unless you can steer yourself from an Incompetent level to a Competent level by being more aware of your thoughts and feelings, on a 24/7 basis as you look at your Life, and as you live it while studying the several emotional and intellectual reactions to your work as Time progresses. Once you have elevated yourself to a Competent Bondage level, you have an opportunity of going beyond this Cycle of Bondage, which is both debilitating and harmful to your long-term progress.

Mental and emotional bondage can be overcome by non-stop awareness, without judgment or criticism of your Life, attitudes and awareness and a deep yearning to live more Happier by improving yourself in relationship to your feeling of Bondage. To improve your Relationship with Bondage, you need to be aware of your thoughts and feelings surrounding Bondage and see how the feeling of despondency and helplessness is feeding into a culmination of depression and dis-taste.

Only with deep contemplation and active introspection can you find the cause of your feeling of loneliness and this awareness and meditation will help you to naturally find a solution to this challenge of isolation, creating a new found Energy which will supplant Bondage with Hope, Confidence and Happiness.

COMPLAINING

Complaining has become a very common pastime. It seems that we need to express our distaste for something by complaining about the qualities surrounding an unfavorable situation. Sometimes our complaints have to do with how others behave towards us, sometimes it is directed towards the actions and behavior of our supervisors at work. In other times, we complain about a negative experience or situation, which has affected us. Will we ever stop complaining??????

Most people do not realize that an active habit of complaining sets up a negative emotional spiral, which ultimately creates a great deal of frustration and unhappiness. Although we hope to improve things or at least, temporarily subside our feelings of frustration and inadequacy by complaining, this habit never really creates any positive results for us in the short or long-term. But the habit, nevertheless, persists and causes more damage than good.

Why do we complain? Have we really gone into this behavior deeply? We desire a certain result or we dream of a certain experience through someone else, whether it be a lover, companion or wife. Such experience does not come to fruition. So our blocked desire, starts the complaining process. We now need to blame someone else for the negative result in our Life. Instead of searching deep down into the causes of the failure in experience or non-fulfillment of desire, we find it very convenient to blame someone else for our misfortune or failure. And can this negative relationship we have with our complaining tendencies be turned around???? It definitely can, once you realize how much harm you are causing yourself and your loved ones by this behavior. When you realize that this relationship with your complaining habit can only create more negative ripples and prevent you from living a fuller and Happier Life, only then will you be able to positively de-construct this tendency.

But any habit is very difficult to modify, since it has taken years and years of practice to behave in a certain way. After behaving negatively for many years, you take the complaining activity for granted and incorporate it as part of your "Living personality," and really do not attempt to change your actions spontaneously. Complaining becomes part and parcel of your living Life and activity and as long as you feel comfortable with your negative behavior, there is no chance of improvement

But through discipline and controlled awareness, you can make a positive step to supplanting complaining with unbiased observations of others you deal and live with. So, instead of finding fault with a Life partner you now focus on finding the right things about her and how the two of you interact. Instead of putting down your employer or office supervisor, you now find ways of celebrating the positive aspects of the relationship.

Do remember that you have two ways to view a glass filled to half its capacity with water: You can view it as half-full and abundant or half-empty and deficient. It is the same glass with the same amount of water. It is your perception of the glass which makes all the difference between a positive attitude or a negative self-complaining behavior. Changing your view towards even a difficult situation can make all the difference between your feeling of fulfillment or non-fulfillment. The more positive you feel about even a challenging situation, the more forces will work to healing the wrongs in it, thereby assuring you a very happy and successful outcome. And is that not what we all choose: to win and succeed in every game of Relationship with relative ease and comfort?????

COURAGE

Courage is the God-given gift to face all Challenges with boldness, confidence and strength. A few individuals are endowed with this great intrinsic quality. However, no one has a Monopoly on Courage. This is a quality which can be developed and enhanced and every Citizen has the right to improve his relationship with the Concept of Courage. Improved understanding and application of Courage will result in superior Life Result in all areas, including work, play and Love. So, how do we conceptualize Courage? How do we see it play a Role in our Lives?

We are exposed to numerous Life stories of Heroes, who defied all human expectation and proceeded to achieve their Dreams by believing in their ideas and value and goals? Do we see ourselves as one of these Heroes today? Probably not. Do we see ourselves becoming a World Hero tomorrow? Of doing something outstanding of which others will not only take note but emulate in order to make the World a better Place? Probably not.

This chapter deals with why we create a bridge or divide between our Performance, Thoughts and Actions as compared with the Lifestyle and values of Heroes, whom we adulate. You create a Bridge, because you perceive you do not have what it takes to Act with Courage in all Challenging areas of your Life. This may be due to lack of self-confidence, lack of self-esteem or simply the Fear of stepping up to do something beyond your comfort zone? Or it might be associated with the intimidatory feeling of not taking on a huge risk to challenge Change and with it, the accompanying fear of losing more than gaining by trying to seek the impossible?

So the first step is to examine your attitude towards Courage. And you cannot attempt this process intelligently without first examining your attitude towards Fear and Accompanying Loss. So if you feel comfortable with your Life, attitudes and actions in spite of lack or diminished capacity of Courage, then so be it. This Chapter is probably of no value to you. But for those, who desire to improve and grow in every aspect of their Life, there must be an acknowledgment and understanding that one has to overcome the Fear of Change and concomitant loss, before understanding Courage. Therefore, the relationship with Courage is best tackled with an acceptance of the Risks involved with Change. And it is only when you open yourself emotionally to the possibility of newness which change accompanies, that you can mould the right attitude and relationship with Courage.

Courage is that unbelievable and all-accepting attitude which moves mountains. Courage allows you to reach the impossible star. Allowing Courage to be part of your Life, by experimenting with new ideas and things, starts you towards a life of Happiness and peace.

Courage also makes the impossible, a very possible affair. All innovation and all growth happens in an atmosphere of Courage and your understanding and ability to conceptualize and internalize Courage will go a long way towards your Success.

CRITICISM

One form of complaining is the dangerous habit of criticism and this behavior deserves special attention. When you criticize, you look down on the other by finding faults in that person. This is usually accompanied by complaining internally about a certain aspect of the other one's personality and behavior. So, when you find fault in another, you criticize their words, actions or attitudes. Such criticism is very demeaning. Unknown to many, criticism also tends to overemphasize your personal ego, at the expense of others. So by putting someone else down, you are strengthening the fact that you are somewhat superior to that person since you do not identify with his characteristics, which deserve criticism.

And then, for those with low self-esteem, there is the constant self-criticism, which is self-defeating. You are putting yourself down by repeating your inability and incompetence in getting the things you feel you desire.

Through this discussion, let me emphasize that there can be a positive criticism process, when accompanied with Love. If you are a physical trainer or manager charged with developing others, you do owe the other one honesty in showing them ways they can improve and engage in peak performance. So in that coaching process, there is bound to be some criticism of the trained. However, if such criticism is performed with a view of enhancing another's performance and not putting them down, then it is a worthwhile exercise. This criticism now becomes a well spring and motivator to peak performance of the trained and if done in a positive, loving way, can assist the other.

However, in many instances, criticism is exercised by someone in a political or business situation, where they have some kind of supervisory or leadership role over you. So how do you understand your attitude towards criticism from such individuals? For one thing, you need to understand that you cannot change the other person's attitude. What you can definitely do is not react to someone else's criticism of you. And you can make an active attempt not to consciously or sub-consciously put someone else down by harsh and unfair words or actions. If you are unhappy with another, try to communicate your displeasure with kind, motivating words. Do not feed your ego or sense of superiority by unnecessary criticism, nor believe you can institute a permanent change in another by criticism. Most criticism leads to long-term resentment and non-cooperation on part of the criticized. See the fallacy of this behavior and attitude.

By changing your relationship with the Act of Criticism you will be a more effective Leader and Communicator and will be able to Achieve more in less time, while contributing to the welfare and progress of those you guide.

DEATH

The concept of Death for most of us, represents an incredible loss of Life. It symbolizes a parting of company with all the worthwhile and important experiences in our Life and a disconnection with our family, friends and surroundings. Therefore, it is not unusual that Death evokes a great sense of fear and foreboding. Not knowing where you are going to after your mortal remains are shed and feeling the extreme fear of uncertainty about any Life after, a person can be driven to psychosis or even suicide contemplating an uncertain future. So how is one to face Life's mystery beyond Death?

Contemporary Western New Age Culture preaches the need to live every moment to its fullest to maximize the experience of Life. It preaches that one needs to stay positive and be courageous as one faces an uncertain future. Although these suggestions are vital to continuing living a healthy and productive Life on Earth, do they go far enough to help an individual understand his relationship with Death?

As one grows older and gets beset with one disease or another, the shortness of Life is intensely witnessed. One looks back and analyzes and discovers what situations and experiences were meaningful and worthwhile---- one also contemplates what relationships and experiences caused the greatest pain. But will this looking back process make one have a better Relationship with Death? Most definitely not.   It seems that one avoids thinking about Death in the Western Culture. In the East, particularly in India, death is viewed as a stepping stone to a new Life and future. Here the Theory of Reincarnation is held in sacred worship by most Hindus. If one were to take this theory seriously, then one would be very concerned about the actions and attitudes undertaken in the current Life, since Hinduism preaches that bad deeds do not go unnoticed or unpunished, whether in this Life or the next. A thief or a criminal, who has stolen from others, will get punished either in this Life or another. But this has somehow not inspired most people worldwide to change their ways.

So how is one to view Death? If you look at this concept very closely, Death represents a termination of all experience and relationship in your present material world. Why is it that we cling to the past and to old memories of pleasurable events and seem to avoid past painful episodes in our Life? Can we not just live right now, in this very second, and enjoy and accept whatever comes our way.

What is the subtle organism, which like a computer, records all events, good and bad, and cross references them with all new experiences? This subtle organism is the Human Mind. The Mind, of course, is doing this non-stop recording and compilation of experiences continually. The Mind is powerful and crucial to our Life on Earth, but it is the same Mind which holds on to happy thoughts and painful experiences and will never let go of this comparison, as one moves through various stages of Life. Our habits and predispositions are part of the protective shell of the Mind referred to as "the Ego", which psychologically represents our safety and comfort zone.

The Ego also lodges the human identity and all the associated conditionings and prejudices. You associate yourself belonging to a particular part of the world, with a distinct affiliation to a specific ethnic group and language and accepted cultural tendencies. Superimposing all of this, is your own particular personality with the various drives, desires and ambition and opinion and pre-dispositions on various matters. This shell referred to as the "I," is the most challenging one of all. As we separate ourselves from others, based on our religious, educational and cultural conditioning, we create a gap or space between the "I" and the they, which refers to everyone outside your interest zone.

So the fundamental question here is, "Can we fulfill our needs and desires, without taking away from another?" And can we approach Life with complete passion and abandon, accepting everything that comes our way, dying to every new experience after it arises. Could we fly like an eagle, which leaves no trace behind of its flight or are we going to imitate a supersonic jet plane, which leaves a trail of smoke and gas behind as it scales the heights of Nature? The life in a jet seems so much more fancier and technologically advanced, but such Life is accompanied with much Pain and fleeting Pleasure.

Your relationship with Death will only mature to Wisdom if living is experienced and simultaneously ended on a moment-to-moment basis. So dying to the known experience, whether good or bad, can happen as soon as the experience is finished. There is no recording or storing of experience. The experiencer is now the experienced. That is it, nothing more and nothing else. Understanding the nature of Death improves the relationship with it. We all mortals have a well-defined physical Life span based on numerous factors. Why not live every moment happily and erase the memory or experience of the moment? Why are we constantly trying to hold on to memorable and excitable experiences and shunning painful moments?

It is possible to live in the moment, like an Eagle, whose flight in yonder Space leaves no trail in the deep blue Sky. This way, Life is ever new and changing and your Heart is always open to new possibilities. In this way, your Relationship with Death is a happy one.

There is a definite possibility of approaching Death more peacefully and positively. But this can only happen when you are willing to die to every experience in this existential moment.

DEBT

Attracting and accumulating Debt is a very debilitating event. In days gone by, our forefathers would teach their children and loved ones to avoid debt as much as possible. Living within one's means was a very important lesson learnt.

But now things have gone totally crazy and out of hand. Western culture, through the intermediary mechanism of credit card companies and banks, and ably assisted by advanced advertising technology encourage people to borrow voraciously. We have now become a culture where it is common place to live with large amounts of debt. So much so that the US has gone into a debt crisis. An average American today is on the hook for around $ 100,000 of unpaid national debt, as a result of his share of the US Government borrowing. Governments are borrowing more and consumers are living beyond their means.

Debt creates insurmountable financial burdens and these can effect the very fabric and quality of an individual's Life. For one, who is indebted to the hilt, such person lacks the ability to think rationally, and is emotionally troubled, unable to focus on a quality Lifestyle with optimum human interaction and relationship. So the question, which begs an answer is, "Why do we humans want to live way beyond our means? Why do we feel we are entitled to a better Car or a fancier Mansion, even though our income does not justify such acquisitions? Why is it important to consume like everyone else? To keep up with the Joneses? For a better experience? For more pleasure? As an escape from boredom?" One wonders how an individual can be really happy with living sanely when there is a constant fear of bill collectors chasing him for unpaid debts or for the matter of his car or house being repossessed? But alas, this behavior of borrowing is now ingrained in the national character and it is very hard to change old habits.

Therefore, one has to understand that the relationship with debt is quite complicated and the more debt one acquires, the more unhappier one becomes. So, there is no easy way of improving your relationship with your personal debt, except by re-organizing your financial Life to only spend up to what you earn, period. Spending 80% of what you get, after tax, is indeed a better strategy. The other 20% can be saved or invested.

The goal of Zero debt is the only and best solution to improving your relationship (with debt). Living a simple Life means paying your bills on time and avoiding financing large ticket items like a house or car, unless your budgets allow for such expenses.

A simple Life will go a long way in overcoming any bad relationship you might have with debt. One needs to beat the debt trap to live a saner financial Life. And without stability in Finances, how can you be really Happy. The common saying, "Money does not bring Happiness by itself, but lack of Money is guaranteed to keep you unhappy," rings true in every instance.

DESIRE

Desire is the wellspring of Life. It fuels and catalyzes most human actions and endeavors. It is very hard to visualize a specific desire or a group of connected desires not being the starting point to get someone moving to from one point to another on the way to achievement of a well intended goal. So how does Desire work? First, it works from a start of expression at a a very basic level---- this level ensures achievement and maintenance of Man's best survival needs. The need for food, water and shelter are all very basic needs and Desire fuels the move to sustaining yourself on Mother Earth. Once your basic needs are taken care of, you then work to getting acceptance and recognition in your Society, followed by the need to fulfill specific desires, like travel, get rich, be successful at work. As you move up the ladder, from basic needs to wishes and desires and then grandiose dreams, you get revved up to move forward by application of your energy. Finally, at the top of the Maslowian pyramid, you have the self-actualized individual, who has, more or less, everything he wants and needs and such an individual lives a totally fulfilled, self-actualized life.

The fundamental philosophical question here is, "Where does one draw the line between need and desire? And how much is enough?" We, as humans, are constantly clashing with others in competitive situations, to extract what we require for fulfillment of our needs and self- imposed desires. For many this is a sum-zero game, where someone's winning entails somebody else's loss in a huge economic system. Very rarely do individuals look at a mutually cooperative economic system where individual gains by a person are swapped for even greater gains to the corporation or clients the individual serves.

The Law of Attraction expounds the boundless abundance in the Universe and the well known fact that there is enough for everyone. For those self-actualized individuals, who have found their true talent and applied themselves in honor of these Attraction Laws, there is the culmination of unbounded benefits to them and their clients, simultaneously.

In terms of the spiritual dimension, too much emphasis on individual desire is an impediment to spiritual progress due to the fact that too much energy is expended in desire fulfillment and there does not seem to be any end to desire; fulfillment of one desire results in replacement by another desire and this cycle goes on endlessly till Man dies.

So what is one to do? How much emphasis should one give to desire? I guess a lot depends on what you really want out of Life. There is no way of escaping the use of desire to fulfill your basic human needs like shelter, food and water. But which desires you tend to focus on depends on a lot of factors.

Every individual has to find what is most important to them. It starts by having a vision of Life and defining your true purpose. Once you have identified your passions and inbuilt talents and chosen an avocation to express yourself, then one must consider to what limit one is willing to go to apply his energy through the field of desires. Is it important to have some quiet time to slow down and be at peace with yourself? Is it important to help others either through charity or in service to others, particularly those who are less bright and more weaker than you? In short, where do you draw the line between your need and desire satisfaction and the ability and willingness to serve others?

A lot really depends on your brand of happiness. Do your current activities and projects give you a deep and abiding sense of satisfaction? Are your personal relationships generating happiness? Are you fulfilled at work? Once you see where you are happiness-wise and where you wish to be, you may need to modify some of your habits and activities to enhance the quality of your Life and re-calibrate your thoughts, feelings and Actions.

The best relationship with desire is to understand that Desire has its own limitations. And that there is no end to Desire. It is also important to accept that there will be times when Desire will get the better of you in terms of extraction of time and energy. Therefore, an individual, has to choose the best balancing Act between Desire fulfillment and his Life purpose. A proper balance between all these competing actors, will help one not only live Life on one's own terms, but also help attract and maintain happiness in Life.

DISSATISFACTION

Have you noticed, at times, a creeping sense of dissatisfaction in your Life? Although things appear to be going well on the Surface, there is a quiet fire brewing within. Accompanying this fear of the unknown, is a sense of dissatisfaction and boredom. It seems something is not quite right, but you cannot always pinpoint the source of such dissatisfaction. This feeling is accompanied by one of inadequacy and your reflection on the apparent inability, on your part, to get what you want out of your Life.

Dissatisfaction can work in either a positive or negative direction. If you view it as a negative, then this will be accompanied by anger, argument and dissension. If, on the other hand, it is viewed as a learning experience, then understanding the root causes of dissatisfaction and creating a way to prod yourself to move forward even faster to reach your goal will create the opposite---- the much desired motion of positive motivation. So which side of the fence are you on? Have you taken the time to think this through? Or are you like most people, who react negatively to poor news and bad experiences and get uplifted by successful outcomes? The choice is yours.

Your own particular relationship with dissatisfaction is based on your own private reactions to the "goings-on," in your Life. What is crucial here is to impartially observe what is transpiring in your Life at this particular point of time. Are you realizing your worthwhile goals? Or not? Are you watching how you mentally and emotionally react when you do not get something you want or need, particularly if that something is held in high esteem by you.

As they say, it is all a matter of Attitude. Improving your relationship with the feeling of dissatisfaction happens when you apply the daily commitment to learn avidly from every experience and goal in your Life. And this approach is armed with a non-yielding attitude to temporary loss or defeat. And a visualization, constantly practiced, that you will get what you want. In this way, you convert the negative seed of dissatisfaction into a happy, positive seed of growth, happiness and prosperity. The keys to this transformation rests solely with you. You are totally responsible for your Happiness or your Sorrow and Negativism. Turn your attitude around and your Life will instantly change. In the process, you will be greeted with much success and achievement.

DOUBT

There are many level of doubt, and all such levels are deleterious to your normal and healthy functioning. Firstly, there is a possibility of participating and entertaining self-doubt. And secondly, there may be a doubt about the longevity of a personal relationship. And finally, there is doubt about your ability to navigate your environment in order to do the things and activities that need to get done to allow you to get what you want. Let us talk about these individual doubts, in detail below.

Self-doubt is comprised of all opinions, thoughts and feelings about your personal inadequacies. Lack of control over your sudden spurts of anger, your emotional uprisings, your feelings of hatred or indifference to others are just some examples of self-doubt. In many instances, self-doubt indicates a lack of self-esteem. To overcome this challenge, one needs to seriously and sincerely look deep inside into the causes of such lack. Positive visualizations, repetitive affirmations and a deep desire to understand the causes of such lack are crucial in your awakening. I would strongly recommend reading, "Psycho-Cybernetics," by Dr. Maxwell Maltz. This book is a wonderful treatise on symptoms, causes and possible solutions to a lack of self- esteem.

Personal relationships mean a whole lot to most people. And attachment in a love relationship or a commitment to a family unit are important reasons for people to be happy and live positively----- therefore the loss of a loved one, or a broken relationship can cause massive destruction to your peace of mind.

If one understands and accepts the temporal nature of Life, with all its ups and downs, its challenges and disappointments, its moments of fleeting happiness and continual pain, one might just look at things differently. If one views the loss of a loved one as a passage into something better or if one views the loss of a beloved, with whom you are engaged (in a close and tight relationship), as a stepping stone to a better opening with someone else, then some of the pain associated with personal loss is dissipated. More dangerous is the tendency to worry about losing an existing relationship in the future; like a spouse walking out on the relationship or your girlfriend finding someone more suitable. This fear of inadequacy can also cause great sorrow and pain. If you can just learn to live in the moment, and give every relationship your best shot, that is all that is important.

The rest will take care of itself as long as you choose not to focus on the loss. This sounds easier said than done, but is very possible with 24/7 awareness of your emotional condition and an unbounded faith that something better is on the horizon for you.

The third major self-doubt has to deal with your inability to adapt and conquer your personal and business environment to get what you want. Human beings are naturally born to be happy, but somehow this natural birthright of happiness is sidetracked and distracted by the numerous environmental pressures one faces. So what starts off as an innocent and well meaning birth transforms into a myriad of external and internal issues, all effecting your level of Happiness and Stability. The Law of Attraction and its diligent practice, will assist in the understanding and control of your reaction to negative forces arising outside you in your personal and business environment. To understand and accept the Power of your Mind, to relish in the possibility that the Mind can wish and get anything it wants and that constant focus and visualization on this intended objective will cause it to be realized in your Life, helps you in moving you closer to the realization of your goals.

Your intelligent relationship with your feelings of inadequacy and doubt are connected to your understanding of this phenomenon. So many of us react needlessly to feelings of doubt--- such reactions involve a sense of despondency, guilt, denial and depression. Instead, it would be far more efficacious if you analyzed the root cause of self-doubt and the source of pain emanating due to this feeling of inadequacy and work with diligent self-awareness to improve yourself.

Improving your relationship with your feelings of self-doubt will go a long way in creating a more Stable, Happy you. And is Happiness not what we all (primarily) seek in our relationships to one's thoughts and feelings? Such Happiness is within the Reach of everyone, provided one approaches thoughts and feelings with a different approach and not just succumb to the emotional reactions to constant feelings of self-doubt.
Step outside the box; be bold enough to see who you are and what troubles you and a new Approach to Life will assist you in banishing all feelings of self-doubt.

ENCOURAGEMENT

To encourage is to motivate. To encourage is to inspire. But alas where is this missing quality? How many people really encourage us to be the very best? Probably, very few. And this is why self-encouragement is the only way to go in terms of assuring yourself a bright future.   Self-encouragement stands for self-motivation, and it involves you constantly encouraging yourself to be better, to giving yourself the permission to think more positively and allowing yourself the ability and Power to garner incredible strength to face Life's winds more successfully.

Many of us depend on others to encourage us on to a better future in the distant. But as long as you look to another for guidance, you permit your Life to be controlled by someone else's whims and fancies. And when that source of encouragement evaporates, you are faced with a void in your Life. Also, the other person, who is encouraging you has his own agenda--- therefore Encouragement is conditional and superficial.

What is your relationship with the general concept of Encouragement? Do you desperately require others, close to you, to move you to climb mountains? Or are you self-reliant? Or are you a combination of both characters? There is no simpler or easier way for lasting Success, than to be totally self-reliant in the encouragement field.

How does one develop the right attitude towards encouragement? Self-motivation is the key, but that is preceded by the understanding and acknowledgment that your Life is yours first and you alone have the responsibility to nurture it. You need to feel that your Success or Failure is entirely within your grasp and you must do the things and perform the mental and emotional actions to attract Success into your Life. And, in addition, you need to craft an overall Life Strategic Plan, accompanied with written Life Goals and a plan of action to get you from where you are to where you want to be. The clearer your Life Goals are, the easier it will be for you to motivate yourself.

Self-encouragement is the key to greater Life Success and your attitude to the relationship between this concept and your Life are crucial to your long-term happiness and stability. Learn and practice the Law of Attraction, read some wonderful books on Goal Setting and Personal Motivation and clearly define and draw your Life goals. Aided with self-encouragement, you can indeed move mountains.

FAILURE

Failure marks your inability, at any point of time, in getting what you want. And there are two types of failure: one is temporary failure, better known or referred to as a "temporary failing," while the other is permanent failure, which is a condition of permanent inability to get what you want. So many times, individuals associate a temporary failure or failing with a permanent failure and this perception causes incredible harm to your long-term probability of Success. And what is Success? Success is something very personal and involves the realization of an individual's pre-determined worthwhile Life goal.

Therefore your relationship with this concept of failure is critical. It is important to understand that temporary failure is almost essential to long-term success. If you do not stretch to get what you want and deal effectively with some short-term setbacks and obstacles, then how can you get what you want in the future? Great salespeople are used to getting hundreds of "No's," when they present a particular product or service to a prospective client, before someone says, "Yes." And the more "No's," you get, the more successful you become. It is a numbers game in the sales field---- more calls lead to more rejections and after the number of rejections to some "Yes's," which leads to more sales. In Life, too, movement towards your goal involves a constant experimentation with numerous "touch-and-go," moments. The crucial part is to keep moving and while maintaining your constant focus on the ball. If you lose that focus, your results either get delayed further into the future or are non-achievable. Having a die-hard attitude, the ability to never let go, to have the confidence that you will win at the end of the day is the key to long-term Success.

Therefore, the right relationship between you and the Concept of Failure is crucial for your long-term Success, Happiness and Stability. If you view a failing as healthy, which results in an urgency to apply more effort and work to reaching your goal, the better it would be for long-term achievement of your Personal and Professional Goals. Remember you are only beaten(you permanently fail) if you say so, and you are always on top if you keep striving, accepting whole-heartedly temporary failings. There is no short cut to reaching the Pinnacle of your Dreams and Goals; there are just small steps you need to take, one a time to move you forward. And do not forget it is the tortoise who always wins the Race of Life and not the Hare.

The tortoise wins because he makes slow and consistent steps towards progress, moving at an even pace as compared to the Hare, which has a short-term outburst of Energy only.

FINANCES

Personal Finance plays a crucial role in every person's Life. So many marriages breakup because of financial difficulty and as a result, innocent young lives, along with what were meaningful relationships get destroyed. The funny part is that to alleviate this situation (and to contribute to more healthier family lives), our universities and colleges have no interest in even teaching a basic course in money management to all students.

Most youngsters are not taught to balance a budget, to project income and expenses and even at the least, start and maintain a savings account. And as such youngsters mature into adults they carry their bad money management habits, which is spending beyond their means, not saving for a rainy day and not setting aside money for future investments. Imagine two people with bad money habits getting together in what promises to be a happy and meaningful marriage and finding they are utterly hopeless in managing their money---- this results in constant fights as to who should spend on what and this ultimately leads to a strained relationship, which metamorphoses in some instances to separation and finally to divorce.

A healthy attitude towards finances is crucial to accumulating wealth or at the minimum keeping your head above water, financially. But if you are not taught these skills at school and college, how are you to have the capability and capacity to learn and apply these skills on your own? This is a very tough proposition with only the smartest kids taking the time and initiative to step "outside the box" with plans to initiating a meaningful savings and investments program and cutting down on credit card bills. It seems the entire North American culture, and its related advertising and social media industry is committed to encouraging citizens to live beyond their means and to spend flagrantly, with no concern for the future. Bankruptcy, ruined relationships and flawed credit ratings are the final result of this behavior. So, if you have not yet given personal and family finances an urgent priority, this is the time to do so. Go back to any college (if you can find one in your area) and complete a basic personal finance course. If you do not have time to go back to study, do an online money management course. Read books on the subject at your local library or bookstore. There are numerous good books on this subject.

Organizing your finances by maintaining a positive, knowledgeable attitude towards your revenue and expense stream will assist you tremendously. The right relationship between you and Money (Finances) will give you the boost to reach your personal, investment and retirement goals more easily and efficiently.

FORGIVENESS

Forgiveness is a much forgotten quality. Jesus Christ preached the value of forgiveness in our relationship with others, particularly with those who wronged us. Mahatma Gandhi, the great sage and freedom fighter from India, said on numerous occasions that if someone slapped you on one cheek, you should offer your second cheek for the same treatment. Here was a person who single-handedly brought down the British colonial rule in India. And he accomplished freedom for India from the cruel, colonial rulers without shooting a single bullet at the adversary. But alas, in our World, there appears to be no place for this wonderful and admirable quality.

Instead, we use anger and violence to express our distaste of someone else's criticism or bad behavior towards us. But, do we stop to ask, if this makes the situation better? By being angry and venomous towards another, you invite more of the same behavior from the other person. And this finally results in mutually harmful, violent behavior. This behavior is not just restricted to individuals; entire nations go to war and innocent lives get compromised due to a perceived feeling or threat to one's way of Life from a distant enemy.

So what is our normal relationship with an attitude of forgiveness? We probably do not give this much thought in our Life. If someone wrongs us in any way, we tend to seek revenge immediately, either in the form of harsh words or violent action. Changing your relationship with the inculcation of a new found attitude of forgiveness is crucial to your mental and emotional health. This does not mean that you do not defend yourself or your values, but just change instantly the attitude with which you exercise your actions. So, is it possible to forgive and yet fight for your cause? It is, absolutely. Forgiveness means sending positive energy towards a person who is sending you negative ripples. It is to pray for his understanding, personal growth and wisdom in order to alleviate your uncomfortable, interpersonal situation. But at the same time, you do what needs to be done to correct the situation. This approach seems a bit contradictory, does it not? But try it.

When you forgive, you release a substantial amount of stress built up in that specific relationship. But by releasing that stress you indirectly accumulate the necessary mental and emotional energy to fight more vigorously for what you believe in, continuing to refuse to compromise on your values.

Seeking and expressing the right approach to negative relationships by constantly adopting a positive attitude to all your actions and forgiving those who have wronged you, while vigorously defending your values will lead to a more healthy and self-composed you.

Even if this approach does not create instant happiness or result, it will relieve you of the unnecessary internal build-up of stress caused by anger and revenge towards one who might have wronged you.

FREEDOM

There are all kinds of human freedom. External freedom is the one most experienced by citizens in developed economies; this is the freedom to express one's view, to vote for a candidate of our choice for political office and the freedom to travel and the right to choose our spouse or significant other. But is this the only type of valued freedom?

And what about Inner Freedom? This is the freedom to explore our inner workings of consciousness and the ability to view our Life and our reactions to various experiences with courage and impartiality. Without this inner freedom, of what long-term purpose is external freedom? Most human beings indulge and draw all their sensations and temporal happiness through external relationships. So, one asks, is the only value of Life having a bigger car, a larger mansion, more cruises and trips and accelerated love affairs and other amorous relationships? Why do we allow our Lives to be circumscribed by such external freedoms? There is absolutely no question that the freedom to move, to travel and express oneself freely is important, but by what token do we ignore our inner selves? Or take this precious Self for granted?

Relationship with your innermost and fundamental freedom, which results in the blessing to be happy is most important. We have gained a great deal in open democratic societies, but there has been very little advancement in inner spiritual growth. And why is this growth important? To live a saner, happier Life where humans can exist in cooperative harmony? Yes, definitely so.

So how does one cultivate the right relationship with this panoramic concept of freedom-- a view which incorporates the right balance between external and inner freedom? I feel, the first step, is to recognize that all the material benefits of the world are not going to make you Happy by themselves. One must also realize that there is an urgent need for self-discovery and realization of a new dimension of Consciousness. Meditation and total 24/7 awareness are the practical devices, which lead one to a new gate, which opens up to Peace and Happiness.

So one must not only grow economically and materially, but also devote one's time and energy in seeking alignment with a Higher Power, which Power possesses an extraordinary ability to heal one's Life and give real meaning and purpose---- one can discover this wellspring, which means to be alignment with the true relationship of Freedom. Freedom must be accompanied by inner Happiness and the dual Purpose can only be achieved through opening oneself to the possibilities of this Higher Consciousness.

Live, laugh and be thrilled in everything you do, but do not forget that there is a deeper Purpose to Life. Come back to that Inner Center, when things get tough or when answers to your daily Life experiences are not enough to bring the Joy in Life, which you may have once experienced.
Cultivating the right attitude towards both External and Inner Freedom are important because in that balance lies true Happiness and Understanding.

FRIENDSHIP

Good friendship showers an important blessing to all those who believe and have good and close associations. Having a circle of close friends, with whom you can share your Life Experiences and rely sometimes for guidance and wisdom is worthwhile as long as you are moving towards the right attitude and approach to Life. Often, the search for close friends is initiated due to fear---- the fear of being alone or not having someone to rely on in the event of emergency. Any movement towards friends due to an obvious lack or fear will not help an individual. Also, any deep association with a group/circle of friends results in the common "value-denominator" of the group influencing your future thoughts, attitudes and actions.

Therefore, choosing your friends wisely is very important. Choosing even a few friends as compared to a large number, who have the will, capacity and determination to uplift and motivate you is important. But creating or being part of such group is a huge challenge. Under no circumstances, should you choose or tolerate "negativity," in your friend circle. Every member in your social friendship circle should try to lift the other to higher positive heights, otherwise what is the need to hide behind a friend network? It is also important to know why someone wants to be your friend. To gain financial favors? Or political favors? Or your influence in getting something they want or need? Friendship flowers most when there is no agenda and the best friends are those who give without necessarily having any expectation of profiting from you. Therefore, the choice of friends is very important.

If you view friendship as a way of not only enjoying the other person's company, but also as a mission to help the other uplift himself then that kind of friendship has the best long-term value. Cultivating the right attitude towards friendship is most important. Serving others, friends or acquaintances, wherever you can will result in your upliftment both materially and in inner well-being.

And what about your "inner friend?" Have you ever pondered about creating a relationship with an Inner Guide? Meditation holds the key to finding a connection with that Inner Pulsating Consciousness, which can now become an Inner Guide and Motivator to assist you in Life's adventure.

The greatest friend is your Inner Friend and if you can create a Social group devoted to advance the causes of Peace, Love and Harmony and a devotion to understanding the Mystery of Life, both Inner and Outer, then you have stepped into a new Spiritual Realm, which source will nourish you in good times and bad.

GLADNESS

How easy is it to be glad all the time? Do you count your blessings, enjoying every moment in gladness on Mother Earth? Or, in reverse, is it not easy to fall into the self-defeating habit of being dull, glum and depressed and constantly critical of others? I guess one has a choice to be at either point of this pendulum---- to choose between gladness and non-gladness.

Gladness, when practiced regularly with total awareness, creates a spiritual stream of Positive Energy. Everything that you now touch becomes whole and poor relationships get transformed into happy ones. Even a difficult, challenging situation becomes lighter emotionally with the application of gladness. On the other side of the pendulum, non-gladness or an unhappiness and unease with your Life and all its resultant experiences, moves you into a negative spiral. Misery does love company and therefore you attract others, who are at the same negative wavelength like you. This creates a further siphoning effect into a negative vortex.

So why is it that we do not count our blessings every moment and every second of our Life? Do we not understand that as we think and feel, so becomes the identical reflection of thoughts and feelings in our Life. Why have we lost our way? Why can we not apply, at every moment, the Mysterious Law of Attraction, which says, "As you think and feel, so do you attract in reality, the mirror image of those thoughts and feelings."

It is very important to examine your attitude and relationship with Gladness. Are you self-actualized in this relationship? Are you aware of how you think and feel, moment to moment? Because, it is only in this awareness, that you can stay on top of the mental and emotional game. Or do you find yourself surrendering to negative emotion at different times during the day.

Nurturing a positive relationship with Gladness, and permitting the Joyful Energy to enter your Life Stream can create wonders for you--- a better, more Happy Self and an ability to enjoy Life to the fullest, while contributing to the welfare of your community and clients.

GOSSIP

Alas, gossip and old women go together or so the story goes. With a dull mind and a mental pre-occupation, accompanied with constant interference and judgment into other people's lives, gossip plays havoc in relationships. Another good example of gossip, is the common habit of "people-watching". This has become a North American pastime. You watch people in public places and then comment internally on their behavior and actions. And the mind delights in such comparisons. It often points out to a false sense of superiority and heightened self-ego. So why has gossip played such a great role in many people's lives? Boredom is one cause. Fault-finding in others is another. And confirmation of your perfection or superiority as you put down others is a third reason.

Gossip does nothing but create negative ripples. Not to say about the needless waste of time and mental/emotional energy. Would this time not be better utilized by just enjoying wherever you may be, without judging, comparing or being critical of others? Why have we not learnt to be quiet? And why can we not just observe everything around us, without judging it? Is it possible to give the ever-chattering Mind a break and relax in choice-less observation? I would encourage you to look at everything in a relaxed, unbiased way. This observation will create the right response to any situation.

Having the right attitude towards gossip, is so important. The disregard of the mental process of gossip will release the much needed energy----- energy which can be applied to fulfilling your Life goals and to the achievement of your dreams. One has only so much energy every day and one must choose where to direct it. A rejected relationship with gossip will help you move further up the Maslowian ladder of needs, with its ultimate goal of having you achieve self-actualization, a stage in which you have everything you want and need, accompanied with much Happiness and Super Heightened Energy.

HONESTY

The wise men have always said that honesty is the best policy. But do we heed their words? There are indeed two levels of honesty: external honesty in your personal and business relationships and inner honesty with yourself. Both need to be working in tandem for maximum success.

Let me elaborate. External honesty deals with communications, attitudes, behavior and actions towards others, including your loved ones, your business associates and acquaintances. So many times, people twist the Truth, in order to enable them to get something from the other without much effort. But this bending of the truth or committing a white lie may haunt them later in the relationship as the deception is perceived by the other. This then results in a lack of trust and a broken relationship.

Inner honesty deals with you being fair with yourself. Do you readily accept and admit your faults and weaknesses? If you do not admit these faults honestly, is there any hope of progress or improvement in your Life? And there is a deep connection between external and inner honesty. In most cases, the two levels of behavior are correlated. If you cheat, misrepresent or bend the truth to get what you want from the other, then this behavior carries forward to your internal assessment of your strengths and weaknesses. You now hallucinate that you are perfect and need to make no internal change to achieve your goals. You therefore start lieing to yourself about your true strengths and weaknesses.

The best attitude to honesty is to believe that this is the only way to live. Honesty is indeed the best policy. You can lie once or twice, but not all the time. And when you get caught in that deceptive role, your credibility and trust go down the toilet in the eyes of the other. In order to grow, you need to be totally honest with all your actions. Presumably, you have established Life goals and have set times, say every quarter, to see how you are progressing towards achievement of these pre-established worthwhile goals. Your complete honesty with your faults and shortcomings as well as with your strengths, will help you move forward. Remember it is focussing on your strengths, while admitting your shortcomings, creates Optimal Life Results.

The right and unwavering attitude towards honesty will result in a better you and much Long Term Success as you fulfill your Life goals.

HOPE

Hope is the everlasting bridge to Success and Happiness. Without Hope, nothing is possible. The human heart has this miraculous yearning for both Peace and Success, and on many occasions, these two goals appear to be incompatible. As one reaches for External Worldly Success, one clashes with forces outside oneself. One is in the process of Change, and Change always invites counter-pressures and counter-resistance. You live in a small apartment and long to have a nice, big home. To reach that goal, you need to save sufficient dollars for a down payment and then reorganize your business and career to generate enough dollars to cover all the payments associated with carrying all the charges associated with maintaining the house. In order to generate that income and wealth, you need to stretch and apply yourself at work to earn that income. In the process of struggle to reach your goal, your Inner Peace does get affected.

You are not really at as much Peace as you would wish. Since Peace is the antithesis of external disturbance, one wonders how one can stay happy within, while struggling in the External World to get what one wants and needs. This alignment process is naturally very taxing and challenging, but nevertheless possible.

Hope is the bridge which connects your External Striving with your Inner Peace. Hope makes you acknowledge that you will reach a point in time, when most of your External needs are fulfilled, then allowing you more time to focus on your inner growth and development. Hope for a better and more peaceful tomorrow, also allows you a to switch off the external pressures daily while you reconnect with your Inner Self. Hope is the flame, which allows you to create that special bridge between the Inner and Outer Life.

How do we normally view Hope? And how do we build a relationship with it? I feel a lot depends on your spiritual and religious orientation. If you believe there is an Almighty Power and further believe that this Power protects you in everything you do, you then utilize Hope as a stepping stone to both future material success and Inner Happiness. Your Hope is powered by your trust in a more omnipotent and Loving Source, an invisible hand, which guides your effort and future Life Results.

Without trust in a Higher Power, it is next to impossible to nourish the seeds of Hope in your Life, long-term. The best approach in your relationship with Hope is to accept it exists to help you grow and that all things are possible when you trust the Universal Energy to work through you to realize your external needs and wishes and at the same time nourish your Inner Being. Hope is the flame which believes in a better tomorrow. Hope is your birthright! Make it work positively for your betterment!!!!!

JEALOUSY

Jealousy is a dangerous yet common human emotion. It burns one's Psyche. So, one wonders about the origin of jealousy. When you study it deeply, Jealousy has its roots in comparison. You live in a small apartment, while your business associate lives in a big house. You drive a small, late model car while your business associate has a spanking new sports car. Your comparison of your material condition with your associate, sparks the emotion of jealousy. You wonder:"Why do I not deserve the same material prosperity as my associate? What makes him so special and I so undeserved?" With this spark of negative emotion, you then tend to despise the other. Hatred and envy go hand in hand and then you conspire to speak negatively about the other. Negativity breeds more resistance and counter-pressure.

Is there a need for jealousy in the World? Is there a need to scorn your neighbor? Is it not possible to believe that there is enough for everyone in the world and that you possess the power and capacity to get whatever you want? Why not learn from your neighbor's Life practice? Why not pick his brains to learn what ideas, values and work practices he employs to become so successful? And pray for his continued success. It is possible to live your Life without jealousy. But this can only be accomplished when there is trust in your ability to grow, utilizing the Power of Attraction.

One must pay close attention to the feelings of jealousy, which come to the emotional surface for most people in different situations in Life. Awareness of the start of Jealousy can result in its sublimation. An intelligent understanding of the deleterious effects of Jealousy will allow you to stop focussing on comparative behavior while positively expanding the thoughts and feelings, which visualize a better future for You. Not allowing jealousy to play a prominent part in your Life, will assist in gathering your Energy for bigger and better things.

The best relationship with Jealousy is no relationship at all. Conquer the feeling of Jealousy, with quiet introspection and 24/7 awareness.

JOY

Joy in Daily Living is what we all aspire to reach. And the pursuit of this spark of Happiness remains the prime source of motivation for Humans. We stretch out trying to accomplish numerous milestones in our Life, but the intended objective of all such action is in the way those accomplishments make us feel. So, unknown and on a highly sub-conscious level, our primary motivator is accomplishment of joy and happiness and we do all sorts of things to reach that exalted state.

But, as we later discover, that Happiness, when achieved, is temporal and fleeting. So, at some point of time, we lose touch with our inner blessing of joy and just focus on getting what we want in the External World, hoping that our level of Happiness will improve with time. We seek that sense of Joy in close relationships with that special partner and our loved ones, like children or family. One thing is for sure----Joy and Happiness, cannot be instantly created nor can it be maintained and prolonged for very extended periods of time. In fact, Joy is a by-product of a different kind of spiritual quality in our consciousness. Joy happens as a by-product of a sane Life, governed with positive values and a sheer sense of service to others, irrespective of what kind of career or business you are in. And it is created and maintained naturally. You cannot force Joy nor can you instantly earn it in your Life.

Through Meditation and inner searchings, one is able to open up a new dimension of Living, where joy and happiness flower. Therefore, the best approach to Joy is to abandon a constant search for its fulfillment in external things; the sensations, possessions and experiences of the External world will never provide long lasting joy. This does not mean that you do not work for what you want and what you believe in. It just means, that you accept that your External Relationships are just one part of a bigger picture. A true Relationship with your Inner Self is all you need to access the fountain of Joy. When you don't fight for Joy, it is there. When you stop getting flustered by all the Change in your External Life, you open up the door for Joy to enter. When you believe Joy is your birthright and choose to stay positive 24/7, you open that secret door to happiness. The best approach in your relationship with Joy is to allow its fragrance in every moment of your Life, irrespective of how hard and challenging your Life may be at this moment. Through a deeper awareness of all your relationships with people, things, ideas and the environment and a quietness and peace in Prayer and Meditation, the spirit and fountain of joy will just appear in your Life.

And is Joy and Happiness not the ultimate goal of all Human Activity? Allow the elixir of Joy to enter your consciousness and your Life will never be the same again.

JUDGMENT

Exercising Judgment is a good or poor method of fully understanding a challenge; it all depends on how you utilize it in specific reference to a situation. Judgment is good when you utilize memory to avoid a situation similar to one which was uncomfortable in the past or avoid associating with a very negative person. In this instance, you use the full power of your Memory to protect your emotions, time and energy. On the other hand, subconscious judgment exercised to reinforce a pre-established conditioning or supportive of an unknown danger or fear can prevent you from exploring new opportunities.

Why and how do we judge? An external stimulus is usually the trigger--- and this can be a chance encounter with a stranger or a heated exchange with a loved one. Instantly and unknown to you, your Mind triggers a reaction to that situation, which is either positive, negative or neutral. It is positive if you feels the encounter will lead to a benefit to yourself or support an already well established internal value. On the other hand, if the encounter results in a memory of a painful situation in the past, you might either shut off or react violently (verbally or otherwise) with the subject in question. You can also have a neutral response, where you do not perceive a threat or benefit from the particular situation.

The exercise of Judgment often becomes a very mechanical, Mind driven process. The Mind being the repository of both good and bad experiences, of both pain and pleasure, quickly decides what position you should take in a situation. If you are in a social encounter, you quickly sum up if the person you are chatting with is a threat or non-meaningful person or if that person says something you believe in, thus creating a tangible benefit to you.

But what if you do not (initially) judge at all in an encounter? Is it possible for your Mind and Heart to be fully open to any message being provided by an encounter? Can you give yourself the chance to fully hear what someone else is trying to say so you get the full length and breadth of the message? And is it possible to consciously suspend judgment, if only for a short while, till the message has been delivered and digested fully? Can you delay your response, both mentally and emotionally to an immediate situation? Being quiet and open to a message, without judgment gives you the opportunity to view a situation polyangularly. Giving some time before reaching a conclusion gives you the depth and maturity to make the right decision in your attitude and response to others.

And sometimes staying quiet and allowing your intuitive Self to give you an answer to the challenge helps.

The right approach to judgment is to exercise it wisely and to withhold an opinion till a calm state of Mind is reached, thus allowing you to move forward wisely and make the right action steps in your approach. And before the action step, too, it is important to see how you are forming opinions and judgments of others quickly. If you suspend the judgment process for a little time and allow your Intuition to take over, the results will be better. You will now become a more open and caring person and one who is not too focussed on what others think about you. Instead you will work on paying complete attention to your own very special private desires and motives and work to attain this without too much attention and criticism from others.

The right relationship with Judgment, is to exercise it judiciously and with complete awareness. Every action has an equal an opposite reaction and every response to experience creates a positive or negative ripple in your consciousness. By withholding judgment early on, and giving yourself the time and opportunity to make a decision in ease, will help in your Pursuit of General Happiness and Success.

LAZINESS

Laziness is normally associated with human inertia, accompanied with a lack of self-motivation. A lazy person has no set Life or Time Agenda, does not wish to move mountains and has accepted the set routine of his Life, however boring and insignificant. And can such a lazy person ever be Happy or Successful?

Where do you personally stand with respect to laziness? Do you find yourself not having the drive to move forward? Or do you view your Life as a series of misadventures and failed enterprises? Or do you lack the confidence to achieve whatever your Heart chooses? As you think, so becomes your Life. This is the famous and most powerful Law in the Universe, "The Law of Attraction." If you change your thoughts, then you can change your Life. But if you lack the motivation to make the necessary changes in your Life, then have you stopped for a moment and asked yourself, "Why am I stopping myself from reaping the rewards of a Happy and complete Life?"

Life is a long and meaningful Adventure and we all possess the key to the kingdom of Happiness and Richness. But alas, less than one per cent of the population are self-actualized, successful individuals. Can you bring yourself to be part of the 1%, in whatever you choose to do? The first step, therefore, is to permanently ban laziness from your Life. But in order to overcome this seemingly huge obstacle, you need to find a way of Living which appeals to you. Choose an avocation of your liking; make goals to achieve your position in this avocation. Set a plan of action for you to get from Point A to Point B, never forgetting your Success will be directly measured by how much you change other People's lives in a positive direction.

The right relationship with laziness is to be aware of the harm this inertia has created in your Life--- this awareness must then be followed by an active attempt to turn around all aspects of your Life to make it more wonderful, positive and dedicated to a cause. And that cause must both be linked to your passion and your ability to help others.

LONELINESS

We all experience Loneliness at different points in our Life. Sometimes the feeling is manageable while at other times, this Loneliness is unbearable and debilitating in our Life. Since our pre-historic cave days, Man tried to find comfort, security and solace by interacting socially with other Humans. In a way, such actions intended to dissipate the feelings of fear and isolation experienced through loneliness. In our modern world, this feeling of loneliness is amplified. Having lost the nuclear family of years gone by and half the nation of many economies enveloped by divorce and separation, Life has truly become a lonely affair.

We live in cages, bound by our physical and mental circumstance. These cages are "golden cages," with all conveniences like internet, television and household comforts but it is still a cage. People in developed societies live together but hardly communicate with each other except when required. So how does one make sense of this Loneliness?

Being Alone is better than being Lonely, although the physical circumstance of each is similar. Being Alone means recognizing and accepting that we all came to this World alone and we will also die alone. It means being at comfort with this algorithm of Life. It means feeling that one can Love without being attached and the clear understanding that one does not necessarily need another person to complete a Life love triangle. It means rejoicing in one being Alone, but all the time staying in positive relationships at Work, Play and in Personal Situations. This concept may sound difficult to understand for most of us, since we have been programmed to believing that a good Life necessarily involves maintaining a presence of a person or significant other at all times to comfort and love us and the presence of a family. Although the issue here is not one of being married or not, or finding love or not, it deals more with understanding and celebrating Aloneness.

And what will lead you to feeling comfortable about Aloneness? It is the cultivation of a spirit of inner awareness, accompanied with a sense of humility and a connection with the Universal Energy which nourishes us. This will help you live in the moment. Therefore, when you are with friends or loved ones, you thoroughly enjoy those moments and when you are with yourself, you are equally at ease. You do not stretch or fight to attract or prolong relationship with a compatible Love partner.

Nor do you engage in needless Social situations to escape from the boredom, which accompanies the feeling of Loneliness.

The right relationship with Loneliness is to understand this is a Poor Life Choice apt to create many negative choices and consequences. And understanding that switching your attitude to one of rejoicing Aloneness in the same Time and Space will reward you with much Peace and happiness. The choice is yours: Loneliness with depression or Aloneness and Happiness. Which one makes more sense to you????

MARRIAGE

To bond our energy with another (in Marriage) is one of the critical decisions we face as Humans. Abhorring loneliness and uncertainty in Love, we strive to create a permanent sense of security through a specific, exclusive relationship. In theory, Marriage constitutes a permanent bond between two partners, who both promise "to live and honor each other till death do us part." So two distinct and separate energies decide to bond together, hoping and praying that this bond will stand the test of Time and Circumstance, through good and bad health, through Fortune and Poverty. Although this is a most wonderful theory supported by numerous religious groups and cultures, in reality it is not always the most efficient form of union.

When we look at the history and result of marriages in North America, we see the national survival rate at 50%; one half of all marriages land up in separation and/or divorce. And what about the other 50%? Are they happy in the relationship or does fear of loneliness and isolation keep them there? So, which side is your bread buttered? Do you choose to be and stay married? Or be in a cohabiting relationship? Or in a dedicated girlfriend/boyfriend situation? Or be celibate?

The choices and alternative avenues around the subject of Marriage are numerous. However, most individuals either marry or cohabit or at the least have an exclusive dedication to their chosen partner. Does this association always work? Yes and No. And where are your thoughts and feelings on this?

There is no perfect answer to this challenge of Marriage. It is solely an individual decision. But to me, what is an important factor and in most instances a determining one, is how happy you are in that specific relationship you have chosen. Does the relationship bring warmth and Joy to your Life? Does it stir you to great heights? Are both of you forgiving of your faults, while still Loving each other?

The right relationship with Marriage is dependent on your desires, needs and goals through this very special association. Being open to a long -term relationship is very healthy, but what form you choose to express this relationship is totally up to your discretion, judgment and experience with your Partner.

Marriage has value if it brings constant meaning and happiness to each Partner; otherwise it is a sheer waste of precious Time and Energy. Only you can decide and implement the best course of action in this vital area of Relationship.

OBEDIENCE

Since times immemorial, we have been taught to follow directives of others, whether these authority figures be our parents, priests or teachers. In simple words, we are told that others have more knowledge of our lives and therefore obedience is a must. By this simple indoctrination, individuals and entire societies have been subservient to the will of authority figures, who attempt to control our thoughts, feelings and actions.

In the Dark Ages in Europe, obedience was directed by way of unflinching loyalty to the kings and queens and a recognition of one's specific social status in Society. As democracy spread through the world, a more subtle form of obedience came into play. This brand of obedience was more tied in to a survival need. In order to survive, a person needed to earn income and if one chose to work for someone else, being obedient and respectful to your work supervisors and management dictates, became a must for job survival.

Now it seems in North America, that although the value of obedience is accepted, there is much freedom to explore ideas and accept or reject them based on how you feel about them. So we have now become an anti-obedience culture, where values are based on peer habits, cultural norms and massive influence by social networking platforms, which manipulate you for commercial purposes.

So what does obedience mean? To me, it means being obedient to your personal values and positivism. It means paying attention to what is most important to you. It also means cultivation of your Mind and Heart to transform you into a more Loving, giving person, who does not only believe in one's own specific needs but is sensitive to the needs of others. Obedience does not mean, fighting with any new controversial idea, which comes out or getting involved in a bitter, argument with another if your ideas or opinions don't match the others.

The right relationship with obedience consists of understanding that Personal, Emotional, Mental, and Spiritual development of a human is most important and if there is any area of obedience, which is worthwhile, then this is through focus on self-obedience to your Positive Values, Goals and intrinsic Connection with Universal Energy.

PEACE

Happiness and Peace is something we all aspire for. However, Peace is a Life Quality, which is hard to discover and even harder to maintain. So, why is it, that we Humans with the most Advanced Technologies and superior brain power fail to experience and sustain Peace? To allow Happiness in our Lives, we need to understand that we cannot use the Mind to gain Peace. The Mind, although a very necessary human instrument without which Survival is impossible cannot lead you into the gate of Happiness. Therefore, one needs to discover if there is a way of entering this area of unbounded Peace, through a non-Mental process.

For most of us, our entire Life and Consciousness is Mental, which is comprised of thoughts, feelings, attitudes, opinions and actions connected with it. So is there a way to give the Mind a break? The very thought of this conjures an image of loneliness, fear and hopelessness. For if we abdicate the Mind, then what do we sense with? Is there a mysterious sixth sense which we have not tapped into? And is it possible to live a life with this Sixth Sense guiding you? The Sixth Sense is the Intuitive One, where information, sensations, directions and actions stem from an unknown Power. This is not engaging in Hallucination or Day dreaming. This Sixth Sense gets activated and energized through heightened periods of Meditation, where one goes beyond the Mind.

You can never capture Peace, but you may invite it into your Life. But the road to Salvation is not through the Mind----it is from a completely different dimension. Peace gushes into your Life in unknown ways and fills your Life with rest, relaxation and harmony.

So to find it, one must abdicate all the known ways of accomplishment of Peace. Man has fooled himself for countless centuries in the quest of Peace. He has tried drugs, alcohol, and religious endeavors, but has failed miserably. Religions have landed up murdering each other's opposing religion members and there have been numerous religious wars in the quest for future Peace and Stability.

To find the real Source of Peace, you need to go on a different journey. You need to be quiet, humble and carry no mental and emotional baggage. Only through this process, is there any chance to attain Peace. You need to keep the windows of Life open to this all pervasive Energy and allow it to enter your Life.

This fresh scent of Love and Happiness may enter in your Present Life or another. But the process of invitation, will change your Life forever.

The right relationship with Peace is not to seek it but invite it in your life. In the meantime, one must live humbly and act positively every moment of your Life. Positivity aids the entrance of Happiness into your Life, but is not a guarantor of such Result.

PERSEVERANCE

Perseverance is a much missed quality in Humans. Perseverance stands for Persistence and no real results in Life can be achieved without this wonderful, but mysterious quality. What most people do not understand is that perseverance can be created towards successful completion of any project or desire. What is usually missing in application of perseverance is a deep Passion towards something and the ability to maintain its strength through Motivation, Visualization and Goal Setting. And most important is the relationship of Perseverance with one's overall Life Purpose. When all these elements of Life Purpose, Motivation, Positive Visualization and Goal Setting are synchronized and integrated then perseverance works miraculously in the fulfillment of your goals.

Persistence means never taking "No," for an answer. It means marching forward in the presence of many disturbances and roadblocks on your path. It means never giving up. It means visualizing attainment of a goal before it actually comes into fruition. As the venerable Dr. Dwayne Dyer announces in his book, "You will see it when you believe in it." And not as most humans who need validation of something through the common failure bound approach, who assert that ' I will believe in it when I see it."

So why is it that most humans do not pay attention to persistence as it relates to their applied strength in various enterprises? For many of us, this is a new concept and way of Living. There are not too many people, who employ these techniques and concepts. So we sink to the lowest common denominator of our social, family and work circle. We tend to more easily attract negativism and entertain reasons why something will not work then attempt to be creative and intelligent in applying new ways of doing things. And for those of us who are adventurous to stick their neck out, they find after a few failures that it is a hopeless cause and therefore return to their old failing ways of doing things.

So how does one make a Quantum Change? By being open in your Heart and Mind to new possibilities. To realize all things are possible with the right amount of effort, prayer and positive visualization. And that persistence will lead the way to your Personal Success.

Your relationship with persistence should be to invite it into your Life in all areas of work, play and relationship. Believing in your cause, while seeing the result in advance of its accomplishment, and applying persistence to all activities and actions will promise you a stellar future and outstanding future Success.

To create Success you need to believe in it first, then let everything else unfold mysteriously towards the fulfillment of your dreams and desires.

SALVATION

For most Christians, Salvation represents the culmination of Life on Earth. As the Bible propounds, in various sayings and verses, Salvation represents a new after Life based on the sins and good deeds you have done. It therefore represents a process of automatic repentance for sins committed and evil acts participated in.

For me, the concept of Salvation is in the Now. One need not repent for anything. Through awareness and a positive attitude, one can change one's way of Life now. The action is always in this moment, and with the right approach, attitude and awareness one harnesses the Power to change one's behavior from your Hellish to Heaven like.

Therefore the challenge is to make a transformation now. We all know and realize we can not change our yesterdays but we can shape our tomorrows through positive action in the present. But alas so few of us live in the moment---- we are constantly oscillating between the past and the future. There is no such thing as living in the Now, This is just a great imagination and deception for most of us. For if you are living in the moment, you would detach yourself from all the opinions, negativisms and pain of the past and just, like a child, approach every situation in the present with the utmost detachment and humility. By detachment, I mean perceiving everything to its fullest extent in the now, without getting memory interfering with your perception. This way you can see everything fresh and untainted in the Now.

Salvation is open to everyone right here and now. Look for that transformation now and you will be blessed with much clarity and wisdom. The right relationship with Salvation is to abandon any religious conditioning with respect to this powerful Word and instead live up to the Challenge of making a transformation now. In this process, aided with Positivism and clear unbiased perception and awareness, one can tap into one's intuitive power to move forward to live a beneficial Life for oneself and ones family, community and the World at Large.

SICKNESS

Sickness represent a dis-ease in our organism. Disease is the other word for this affliction. Something in our physical, mental, emotional and spiritual system does not jive and sickness is the symptom of this imbalance. We pay so much attention to the symptoms of this malady. Billions of dollars are spent in North America on all kinds of pain killers and stress busters, but the doctors and other experts never go into the depth of the problem. It is also about temporal relief.

The opiod crisis in the developed world is a direct reflection of this malady. People find it difficult to adjust to the constantly changing demands of Life, as some may not be able to live within their financial means, while others experience family and children issues. And pain follows. For some it is physical pain, for others it is mental anguish and for most of the afflicted, it is a combination of both physical and emotional pain. In order to avoid and escape this pain, one may resort to drug use. It seems a good temporary escape, but when the effects of the opiod vanish you are back to where you started and now need more opiod. This starts the cycle of drug dependence. This devastating cycle of drug abuse has resulted in thousands of deaths every year in North America. But has anyone tried to address the root cause of this malady? I do not believe so.

How are you going to change this all? First by taking care of your nutrition, eating just enough and the right chemical quantity of food (balanced diet of protein, carbohydrate and fat). Secondly, exercising every day, even for twenty to twenty five minutes. Then working on your inner self through meditation and 24/7 awareness. Learning how to apply the Law Of Attraction, aided with positive thinking is helpful. Then sitting down and developing your Life goal and instilling a sense of purpose in your Life and working towards fulfillment of that purpose.

The best relationship with Sickness is to first realize it is not necessary. And secondly, to institute a nutrition, exercise, meditation, positive thinking and Purpose of Life exercise to focus on what you really want. Through this process you stand a wonderful opportunity to release pain from your System and live a long, healthy and pain-free Life.

SORROW

Life is filled with so much Sorrow, that this is just unbelievable. We get caught in our routines, but do not find much happiness there. Although we pretend in front of others, to be ok and happy, this is never really the case. Life seems to be punctuated by periods of boredom and monotony, interspersed with few moments of calmness, peace and happiness. Sorrow and resultant pain seem the dominant theme in our World. Most of us do not accept this theory, but if you observe yourself honestly, this is what truly happens.

So what is Sorrow? And what does it indicate? The Great Gautama Buddha, one of the enlightened souls of the East, preached long and hard in India and what is now, parts of China and S.Asia. His message showed that sorrow was the price humans paid for unacceptable and unwise thoughts, actions and feelings. And Gautama said that the only way to change all this was to conduct life in a different optimum way. In his 8 fold way of Action in Life, he propounded the important elements of this Path. In a similar way, but in a different time, Jesus Christ also propounded the essential Principles of Life through publication of the 10 Commandments.

Setting aside for a moment what the Great Spiritual Masters have propounded about mastering Sorrow, have you asked yourself if you have seen and for the moment, accepted the Sorrow in your Life? Have you tried to study the origin of Sorrow and its cause as it effects your Life? And what steps are you taking to alleviate the situation?

The ending of Sorrow is your Human Birthright and one must work long and hard to diligently study all sources of Sorrow with a view to eliminating it completely from your Life. The right relationship with Sorrow is your intent to annihilate it, through observation and unbiased perception, thereby creating a better, more Positive, Happier Life for yourself and your family.

It is possible to end Sorrow, but you need to gather your energy and Motivation to surpass the normal, monotony and repetition of your Mind activities and replace it with quietness, understanding and poly-angular attention. And most important, you must trust the Wise, Intuitive Source to nourish your Life with Peace and Humility, a condition in which Sorrow cannot exist.

STRESS

Stress is something we all humans experience. What makes the difference is the reaction to stress which varies from person to person. One person may thrive under the most stressful situations, while another person may go bonkers.

So what is Stress? What is its origin? And how can one live Life in the presence of stress, while not being affected by it? Stress has both psychological and physical roots. And one has to be aware of the symptoms of stress, before one can proceed to investigate its source. One likely symptom is the feeling that the world around you is not good and/or a feeling of boredom with your normal activities. This is an emotional maladjustment symptom which needs to be noted. The symptom then points to a deeper cause, which then needs to be investigated. Or you might have a physical malady like high blood pressure, migraines or other symptoms, which point to alleviated stress. On the other hand, the symptoms may be rooted in a physical deficiency or issue, like high blood sugar or a weak heart or liver.

Once you determine where the stressor is, you can then take steps to get rid of it. The stressor may still exist in the environment, but what changes is your attitude to it. If you see it in your job, business or career and know there is no way of getting around it, you have to just modify your attitude towards it. For example, if you are a top flight salesperson, and know you have to hit goals every month, and that the goal deadline is a stressor, which is going to stay as long as you are in that profession you modify your attitude to get yourself in peak performance, while working to keep yourself fit physically, and finding healthy outlets for your stress like indulging in hobbies, physical fitness, etcetera. You could also distract yourself by giving yourself small rewards every time a sales goal is reached. Stress is a major detractor to human productivity. It causes billions of dollars of loss in the economy, as a result of loss worker productivity, due to absence from work. The best relationship with Stress is to understand it openly and honestly; to spend the time to be aware of its beginnings and deleterious effects; to institute a program of physical fitness and mental recreation to stay on top of the stressor. Stress is present everywhere but you relationship with this phenomenon consists of actively trying to tone up your physical, mental and emotional faculties to deal with it so that you win in spite of Stress---- never allowing it to take away from your precious Life or your relationships.

TEMPTATION

Temptation in the Biblical perspective points out the first existence of Man on Earth, where the Good Lord provided Adam and Eve, with everything they could possibly need and want to live happily. However, the Lord warned that one special tree was out of bounds for them. As the story goes, the serpent (which is representative of evil), tempted Eve to fetch an apple from this particular banned tree. On having disobeyed the Godly directive, Adam and Eve were banned from their garden and home in Eden. The moral of the story is that a Human succumbs to temptation and the consequences of such action are disastrous.

The significance and impact of Temptation in our Personal Lives, go beyond this narrative. Greed and avarice, the need to break rules to get ahead economically, constant lies and manipulation to extract money from an unwitting public are all examples of how some men steal from others to get ahead financially, socially and politically. Temptation therefore is a negative personality trait, closely connected to Human greed and avarice, leading to thievery and lies.

So what is one to do? First one must recognize that negative tendencies of temptation abound in our relationships and there is a need to protect oneself from such agents in the environment. Secondly, one must search deep inside to see if pockets of temptation exist in oneself individually and take steps not to move in the direction of the temptation.

The relationship between you and temptation, is to study the onset and movement of temptation, never allowing yourself to go towards this wrong path---- to control wisely the urge to gain from others, by systematically employing deception, blackmail and lies. It is also important to recognize and accept that there is enough resource for everyone's need and wish in this World. This recognition will deter one from thinking or acting in a way of belief, which supports the application of Temptation to get ahead. If you realize there is no long term progress or positive result through temptation, then you are truly a Wise man. There may be instant gratification and initial success but temptation will never create the right and ethical direction to move forward in your Life.

UNCERTAINTY

Uncertainty as expressed through any thought, feeling or Action is looked down upon by contemporary Society. On the other hand, decisiveness is much celebrated. There seems to be a particular well accepted Thought process by most people, which says that the successful people in the world are those who are extremely decisive and great risk takers. And that all others who exhibit uncertainty are not to be taken seriously; they are merely tolerated as an insignificant part of the cultural fabric.

Psychological uncertainty is a great virtue, because it indicates an active and examining Mind. It is a sign of wisdom, where decisions are not made solely on your intellectual understanding of a true or current event. Uncertainty supports the investigative process and give one adequate time to consider the options available to best solve an external challenge. The danger around Uncertainty is the fact that prolonged uncertainty on any matter could cause very negative consequences. But as long as one is aware of the short-term benefits of uncertainty, one can use the initial time after onset of a Challenge to actively investigate all the possibilities for effective decision making, later firming up a decision within a certain fixed period of time.

The best relationship with uncertainty is to be able to use it constructively to determine valuable Life decisions to help you to get to where you want to go. Some fixed and predetermined time for meditation on the actual Life challenge followed by a decision and then action will move one more optimally towards fulfillment of one's predetermined Life goal.

WORK

Work has so many different meanings to people. For most of us, work is a means to physical survival. Without an income, how is one to pay for all one's basic needs? How would one pay rent or a mortgage, one's electricity or phone bill? Or buy food and other Life necessities? It would be utterly impossible without Income. And to earn income, one either needs to have inherited wealth or work in a job or business to generate cash to pay your essential bills. So, most of us, swap an incredible portion of our Life, Time and Energy, in exchange for a wage. And most of us actively work till we are at least 65 years old, when we are presented, if fortunate, with a gold watch from our employer to commemorate our retirement. What a tragedy of Life!!!! And there are those trailblazers, who are born entrepreneurs, who have taken great risks to start a business and have become incredibly successful financially.

Where do you personally fit in with respect to this whole challenge of Work? What does work mean to you? Why do you slave 40 hours a week for 40 years? To put food on the table? To get rich? To be personally fulfilled? Most of us do not look initially at fulfilling ourselves through Life's work. It seems we get caught up in the drudgery and routine of a job or business, knowing it is generating a certain amount of money to take care of our minimal needs. Lost is the process of self-discovery into focusing on your real strengths and passions and finding a way of investing those qualities into work.

To me, the most important challenge is to find your passion and then express this passion through a corresponding work. This will guarantee you incredible success in any field you choose. To work just to put bread on the table, will not motivate you long-term. It will instead create a sense of boredom, long-term, and all kinds of negative stress reactions, both psychological and physical. Accompanied with your passion must be your desire to serve others. If you simply focus on giving your clients the best advise regarding selection of products and services and follow up to fulfill their needs on a regular basis you will be incredibly successful. Your best relationship with work is to meet positively the challenge of finding work, which you feel most passionate about and which is commensurate to your natural and technical skills. And helping others superlatively in your chosen work, will add to your Success.

We all need to Work – why not work with Passion, Love and a Spirit of Service to your Clients??? Armed with the Law of Attractions, Goal Setting, Institution of a Plan of Action and Constant Motivation, you can now have the best relationship and success in your chosen work.

PAGE LEFT BLANK INTENTIONALLY

PART 2

DISCOVERING THE SPIRIT WITHIN
-YOUR JOURNEY BACK HOME

FINDING TRUE LOVE

Finding true Love is one of the toughest challenges in Life. For Love has so many meanings and connotations. We humans strive to find Love through an External Relationship, while ignoring who we are and how we relate to our inner self towards others. All Love starts with Self-Love, because if you cannot love yourself, then how can you find meaning with another? If you hate yourself or your Life, then how can you find satisfaction and fulfillment in another? You project silently who and what you are. And negative reflects on the other and creates a double negative effect. A restless soul with great anxiety and unfulfilled desires can create havoc in a relationship. So self-love first, with a healthy caring attitude towards others is the first prerequisite for successful Love--- a love which not only enriches the other, but is also representative of your intense self-love and positivism. A person who is a High energy type and happy and loving can project that energy in a room, even without opening his mouth. Energy is a powerful and invisible aspect of Life.

So before you go out seeking Love, have you first taken the time and thought to truly understand your nature, personality and values? Do you have a high level of self-esteem? Can you control your anger and other negative impulses? Can you be kind and patient with yourself? Because without the cultivation of these qualities, you cannot touch the other positively. Negativism in one person breeds negativism in the other and the Love Relationship will eventually fail.

And what about the most important relationship of all? Your relationship with the All Abounding Universal Energy. Are you aware of the Power of this Infinite Energy? Do you touch and feel this Energy on a warm sunny day and honor this benevolence (equally) on a quiet moonlit night? Do you admire with abandon, the vast mystery of the Universe on a clear starry night? Do you feel the beauty of all the planets and solar systems around us?

Being open to this universal energy invites Love and Peace into your Life. But alas the mind is never quiet. It is truly a "bumble bee," keeping you occupied in so many projects, big and small. And by the time you have sufficient time and energy to devote to finding yourself, you are too old and weak. The real challenge to finding Love is to invite this universal energy 24/7. Love and humility work together.

So appreciation of the Universal Energy, a deep understanding of your intrinsic traits and quirks and a humility based on meditative contemplation will help you find Love everywhere.

Love is not necessarily confined to a one-on-one relationship, although those who attain that happiness (there) are indeed blessed. Love is impersonal and abundant in all your relationships with ideas, things, People and Nature. Love means being kind and helpful to others knowing that there is always enough for everyone. Finding the right way to Live through Love remains one of the challenges for Man. For without Love, what is Life worth?

SPIRITUALITY

What is this dimension of Consciousness we associate to Spirituality? And is this unknown medium accessible to all? And in reality, how many of us live in this dimension?

First, let us understand what Consciousness is. The energy, which moves us psychologically, as expressed through thoughts and feelings comprise part of the Great Energy swirling through our human organism. Consciousness is the sum total of human energy, both psychological and physical. Consciousness is represented by the powerful surge of Energy which powers Humans. Without it, all is lost. There is no concept of Existence without movement of Energy and Consciousness describes and circumscribes Human Life on Earth.

How we tap our Consciousness and re-direct it towards Universal Energy marks the difference between a mundane Life and a Spiritual Existence. The Spirit exists where the Mind is not and to enter this Realm one needs to travel light. The kingdom of Heaven is unknown to most of us. Very few individuals ascend to this highest level of Spirituality.

So how is an ordinary person with an extraordinary vision and desire for growth to tap into this Spiritual Consciousness? One starts necessarily with meditation, knowing that Thought has its use and place in Human Life, but that transcending your earthly "Thought" vision is necessary to go beyond this mundane psychological activity.

The Mind is a wonderful servant but a dangerous Master and existing subtly on the other side of the fence is the "Spirit"-----which side of the fence you are on ultimately determines your Spiritual Future. This journey towards the Spirit is an incredibly personal one and a seeker must search and find and develop the ultimate level of consciousness best suited to his needs. But to get to this gate of Super-consciousness, one needs to be humble and quiet and introspective, viewing every situation within and without with poly-angular attention.

It is only when the Mind is quiet that it can reflect back on itself in its relationship with the World at large and in its attitude to various Life relationships. Such a quiet Mind is a temple of blessings, and creates an opening into the quiet space of the unknown.

Spirituality blended with right and purposeful living is the evolutionary path we all humans are on. And eventually the Peace and Existence of this Planet will be based on whether we, as humane co-existing on Mother Earth, can nurture our souls and learn to live with each other more co-operatively.

Spirituality is a birthright of Humans, but alas this energy is not tapped by most of us, resulting in confusion, anxiety and much Pain and Unhappiness.

MINDLESSNESS-THE NO MIND ZONE

It seems that we humans are incessantly caught up in Mind Activity. By this I mean that we reflect on our life, that we see the appearance of our Experiences being like a rolling circus filled with numerous thoughts, feelings, attitudes and opinions on a vast and diverse area of subjects. As we grow from infancy to childhood to adult Life, we take these thoughts and feelings as the only way to live Life, for want of knowing any other way to Live.

So, depending on where you are born in this beautiful Mother Earth and parental influences and genetic conditions, one individually chooses and prescribes a retain model of psychological activity. And as time progresses, we tend to believe that this mental activity is normal to us--- it is very private and through this process we develop an individual identity.

Unknown to us, is a vast and mysterious Life beyond Thought. Thought merely represents the response of memory to the past, and its projection into the future. There is no such thing as living in the present, although we are all aware of this saying. So the Mind, with its incredible power and movement is constantly reacting to external and internal stimuli, and creating a yarn of dreams, imaginations, hopes and desires. And as we progress through Life and Old age, this represents the sum total of our Life. Our Life is nothing more than the sum total of our experiences, which comprise additionally our reaction to Life moving events.

So even trying to step out of the Mind Zone, is incredibly difficult for most of us. This is why Meditation is such a Challenge, when done properly. For the Mind wants to maintain control of your consciousness at all times, so quiet Mindless meditation throws out tremendous fear and insecurity. If one steps outside one's bubble and examines this fear, one realizes it is a way of the Mind asking you to stay within a certain psychological zone of activity.

It is only when you step outside the dictates of your Mind, through Mindless and choice-less awareness, that you can enter the Kingdom of the Spirit. Such detached and aloof awareness of your thoughts, feelings and attitudes now opens up a new door of Intuitive understanding, which then helps clarify difficult Life situations and gives you a glimpse to a better and more purposeful Life.

Mindless meditation is the opening to this Sacred Gate of Consciousness

MEDITATION

Meditation is the first and last gateway to a new Consciousness in Man. However, the word, "Meditation," means so many different things to people-- its meaning and interpretation also changes from one part of the world to another. In the West, Meditation is associated with a technique or process of stress release and reduction. But is this the meaning of Meditation? And is this its real purpose? Is Meditation the same as Prayer and Positive Thought? Or is it something which exists in a No-Mind Zone?

The only purpose of Meditation is to reach and operate from a Higher Level of Consciousness. This Higher Level has nothing to do with the Mind---- in fact it only exists when the Mind is not. This explanation of Meditation is very new to most people. It seems one's entire Life is circumscribed by Thoughts, feelings and opinions of a very private nature and it becomes difficult for anyone to imagine a Life devoid of such experiences and attitudes. One lives entirely inside one's own private "bubble."

This bubble is comprised of all the pre-concieved notions of self- identity and self-value. Inside this bubble is also all the pain associated with past experience and the memory of fleeting happiness encountered through Life's journey. Can you risk looking at Life in a new fresh way???? Can you live without Thinking, even if this is for a short while? The thoughts of Meditative practice do indeed frighten a lot of People. But this is the Challenge--- nothing ventured and nothing gained now is the answer to your Fear of jumping into the Unknown Energy field of No Mind.

The challenge of Meditation is to give yourself the temporary permission to risk jumping into the unknown---- thereby allowing yourself the opportunity to enter a new field of Spiritual experience. And to get into this high intensity Energy vortex, one needs to travel light. One needs to abandon, if for that moment of meditation, all of one's past experiences and opinions. It is only such quietened Mind state, which allows the end of interference of perception of the Unknown. And so, how does quieten one's Mind? Most social systems of learning propound quietening of the Mind as something associated with repressing certain thoughts and feelings? Or superimposing the chattering Mind's thoughts with a religious or indoctrinated system of approach. Nothing is further from the Truth. To experience the full value of Meditation, one needs to have the right reason and purpose for such Exercise.

If the only purpose of Meditation is to get temporary relief of stress or thought afflictions, then it may serve that objective well. But once you are out of that Meditative mood, you go back to where you started with: a confused Mind, driven by numerous unfulfilled desires. However, if your true Purpose is to understand, with total unbiased observation, the wonderment of the Spirit and your relationship with it, then you embark on a longer journey of self-investigation and study.

Meditation starts very simply. In simple and unambiguous words, it is the cultivation of total 24/7 awareness of everything within and without you. And such awareness must be necessarily accompanied with no judgment or criticism of what you see. In the process, you build a field of consciousness, untouched by Thought. This new field, with time, becomes very strong and energetic. It is truly a magnetic field, which attracts a different level of consciousness. But are you up to this vast and mysterious Journey???? Are you willing, even for a short period of time, abdicate your association with all your pre-conceived pre-disposiitons, ego and set thoughts and attitudes on almost everything in Life??? Can you make a commitment to yourself to stop the Thought Process, even for a short while? Can you be aware of your thoughts and feelings, but not participate in them? Can you employ the power of Awareness to create that Space between You and Your Bubble, comprising of all your thoughts and feelings experienced at a certain moment of time? This, to most, appears to be an arduous and sometimes impossible process. But for those, who seek greater value of their Life and a deeper inquiry into their Purpose there appears to be the appearance of an unbounded Strength and Energy guiding them to discover a new Spirit, With this practice and non-stop Awareness, comes the Attraction of unbounded love, Grace and Energy. And this is accompanied with much Happiness.

Meditation offers the gateway to a new way of Living and a special form of Happiness. This Happiness cannot be prejudged or self-projected. It is a natural form of Happiness. And is Happiness and Love the predominant need of Mankind?????? So often, we feel we have found Happiness, but realize at the end, that this was merely illusory. Meditation, when properly practiced, creates a new Permanent Zone of great Happiness and Love.

MEDITATION 2- SIMPLE BEGINNINGS

A great start towards a meditative practice is to sit quietly in a favorite place in your Home or Office. Try to be surrounded with no distraction. Turn your cell phone off. Shut your music receiver. And be far away from your TV set. In that quiet, undisturbed state become an aloof observer of all your thoughts and feelings. As you shut your eyes, you witness a myriad of thoughts and feelings. The Mind is still active as it role plays and recollects significant experiences of the Past and reviews challenges ahead. As you close your eyes, do not allow yourself to drift into amplification of any of you oncoming thoughts or feelings. Just watch everything silently. In the beginning, this will be hard to accomplish, since you have established a set psychological pattern of thinking and reacting to different events.

Should you find your Mind stray from your choice-less observation, then be aware of your allowed wandering. That awareness of a drift, will automatically bring you back to your "No-Mind" Center. Stay in that center as long as you can. As you grow your practice from a few minutes to a few hours of awareness, you will feel the presence of a New Energy. This Energy will be drawn from a different level of consciousness. Now this Energy will bring much clarity and direction in your Life.

If you have further interest in the subject of Meditation, the author suggests you read his forthcoming book entitled, "Unconditional Meditation." This book goes into much more detail on how Meditation works to create a Peaceful Zone and also described impediments to a Life of Humility and Grace.

POLY-ANGULAR ATTENTION

Attention can be focussed on a specific subject or it can be diffused. In one's personal, career and work ventures, it is highly advantageous to focus your attention and Energy in a specific manner to achieve pre-conceived result---- but is it necessary to have the same focus on matters of the Spirit??? Poly-angular attention is the only way one can get close to the Spirit.

What is this type of Attention? "Poly-angular" necessarily means looking at everything simultaneously with varying angles of observation? It also means not distinguishing your personal thoughts and feelings from other events happening simultaneously around your Life at any moment in Time.

So when you walk in your favorite park, you pay as much attention to Nature around you as you focus on your inner Thoughts and feelings. Meditation therefore comprises of an openness to every moment within and without. You are as attuned to your inner feelings as you are to the beautiful bird singing away in abandon. You are, at the same point of time, also receptive to and aware of the beautiful flowers in the garden while you do not ignore the mysterious breeze floating through the park, giving you much fresh air and blessing. Everything is included in your Meditation. This is true Meditation and it necessarily involves the employment of poly-angular attention.

When you are sitting quietly in your room, practicing Meditation, you again employ poly-angular attention by being totally open to all thoughts and feelings within and without and any movement outside you. This level of attention invites contact and acceptance with everything on a 24/7 basis. Understanding and application of poly-angular attention assists in acceleration of Spiritual development and invites the scent of Life to enter your system to create much Love and Happiness.

INTUITIVE INTELLIGENCE

Intuitive intelligence is that spark of Divinity from within and without. It comes on its own with no aid or forewarning. And to allow it into your Life requires a deep sense of humility. So what is Intuitive Intelligence?

We humans operate at different levels of Intelligence. And such intelligence is in many instances conditioned. In the East, deep superstition and religious conditioning influence the final decision making process in any Life Activity. In the West, although there are deep pockets of religious conditioning, most decisions happen through rational intelligence application. It seems that wherever you go, most Humans support and stand behind their decision making processes, whether right or wrong. They also support their application of intelligence in such decision making process. Therefore, Intuitive intelligence appears to be a foreign concept for most Humans right through the world. They seem to have no clue as to what it is, how to invite it into their Life. For many, it appears to be an esoteric concept to be deeply feared and avoided at any cost.

Intuitive intelligence is a source of Power way beyond the accumulated knowledge or conditioning of most cultures. It is a mysterious source of Direction for someone, who is willing to submit to forces beyond his normal understanding. This does not mean that you stray from logical and rational observation, analysis and decision making. For example, there are so many times in one's Life, when one is faced with a tough decision making process, since two or more options all appear to be as worthwhile. So what does one do here? Faith and Prayer are most important here. To understand and accept that there is an All Knowing Source around us which can provide guidance in challenging times is a must. And to constantly Pray to find the right road of Life is important, knowing that guidance will always come if you are open to it. So Intuitive Intelligence is the all knowing Source of Energy which guides you.

How one distinguishes between a Mind-driven decision and an Intuitive Mysterious one is a real challenge on more than one occasion. Usually this intuitive flash of understanding comes quite automatically, and can be distinguished from a Mind-sourced decision. Intuitive Guidance appears through a sudden flash of awareness and understanding and is of great assistance in challenging Life situations.

The same Intuitive Intelligence can be your guide in your investigation of your inner spiritual core. To be silent, open and accepting of this great Power and to allow it to touch your Life will create a more perfect, blissful and happy Life, a Life in which you face your circumstances courageously knowing there is a Greater Power to guide you.

Meditation with poly-angular attention assists in opening up the Inner Space for the advent of Intuitive Guidance and Intelligence.

CONCLUSION

VIOLENCE OR PEACE: OUR ONLY 2 OPTIONS ON MOTHER EARTH

The history of civilization has been filled with much violence and unhappiness. As Man evolved from primarily a jungle living animal to a technologically advanced entity, there appeared to be no real deep Spiritual Change. Monarchies have been replaced with democratic states (and socialism and communist rule, in isolated pockets), but nothing has really changed. "The spear" of our pre-historic ancestors has now been replaced by weapons of mass destruction, weapons so powerful that they can wipe out entire countries at a moment's notice.

- We therefore have this incredible challenge to either live together in Peace or destroy the very fabric of our Life through war and violence. But we do have a choice. Mankind is at the edge of spiritual change and it is only this change, which can bring order and peace in the World. We must all learn to live together in Peace and Harmony and share our resources so that poverty is eliminated, income equality erased and brotherhood grows.

- Spirituality is the key to help Man come together with Man. The alternate is total misery and annihilation of the World. If only we took the time to study the history of civilization and how in the name of religion, country and belief we have killed each other aimlessly, will there be an opening to a new way of Living. Meditation, awareness of the needs of the other is most important in crafting a better Life for all.

- We do have the option to improve our Lives but not at the expense of the other. Co-operative spiritual living, where everyone helps the other is a possibility. It is the author's fervent prayer that this way of Living is created, so that Man learns from all his mistakes of the past and creates a strong, meditative zone of Energy where there is Prosperity for all. It is only through helping others that we can grow long-term as a human race and we need more and more spiritual leadership to guide us onwards towards this path.

- This path is totally possible and within our reach. The meditative movement has already started all over the world and we are at an inflection point---- more spiritual growth or anarchy and violence.

- We possess the power to make the World a better place, through Meditation, utilization of the Power of Positive Thinking and our employment of Faith and Prayer in our ability to attract and maintain good and defeat the forces of greed, avarice and violence.

- Every human being holds the key to a better Life and the author believes that we will make a Peaceful and Permanent transition to a better and blessed Life for all.

www.ingramcontent.com/pod-product-compliance
Lightning Source LLC
LaVergne TN
LVHW081334060426
835513LV00014B/1280